Lecture Notes in Computer Science

Lecture Notes in Computer Science

Edited by G. Goos and J. Hartmanis

404

Joachim Beer

Concepts, Design, and Performance Analysis of a Parallel Prolog Machine

Springer-Verlag

Berlin Heidelberg New York London Paris Tokyo Hong Kong

Author

Joachim Beer
International Computer Science Institute
1947 Center Street, Berkeley, CA 94707, USA

CR Subject Classification (1987): C.1.2, D.3, I.2.5

ISBN 3-540-52053-8 Springer-Verlag Berlin Heidelberg New York
ISBN 0-387-52053-8 Springer-Verlag New York Berlin Heidelberg

Printing and binding: Druckhaus Beltz, Hemsbach/Bergstr.
2145/3140-543210 – Printed on acid-free paper

Preface

The research presented in this thesis was carried out in conjunction with a joint research project between the GMD - Research Center for Innovative Computer Systems and Computer Technology at the Technical University Berlin, the University of Kaiserslautern, NIXDORF Computer AG, and Epsilon GmbH.

Of all the people involved in this research project I owe the most to Professor Dr.-Ing. W.K. Giloi who trusted me enough to let me lead a research group at the GMD-FIRST even though I was a newcomer to his institute. He also showed enough faith in my ideas to let me go on when others had their doubts.

I also wish to acknowledge the support of all my colleagues during the time this work was done. I would especially like to express my gratitude to Mrs. G. Tysper and Mr. Abel who helped me tremendously with the administrative duties a project leader has to live with. I gratefully acknowledge many discussions with the scientists and engineers from the other research partners who always showed a keen interest in my work.

This project was funded by the German Ministry of Research and Technology (BMFT) and NIXDORF Computer AG to whom I express my gratitude for their financial support.

Last but not least I would like to thank my wife and my little son for their support and their understanding when daddy could not take them to the playground but had to work.

Berkeley, October 1989   Joachim Beer

Contents

1 Introduction

1.1 Outline of the Thesis

This thesis is the account of the design of a high performance parallel Prolog machine for *sequential* Prolog. This work is, therefore, not about the development of yet another parallel Prolog dialect, or even about language extensions to Prolog to facilitate parallel processing. The primary objective was the design of an architecture that allows for the parallel execution of *sequential* Prolog. However, in contrast to other attempts to execute sequential Prolog in parallel, I do not restrict the use of any of the standard Prolog language features such as dynamic assert/retract, CUT, etc..

Because there is very little empirical knowledge about how much parallelism existing Prolog programs exhibit it had to be guaranteed that the desire to exploit parallelism does not result in a performance deterioration for those Prolog programs that do not exhibit *any* kind of parallelism, i.e. completely sequential and deterministic programs. It is certainly true that the amount of parallelism in Prolog programs depends on the application domain as well as programming style. However, the fact remains that there is a large body of existing Prolog programs that have been programmed 'sequentially', without any regard to parallelism. And those programs have to be supported too.

Even though the architecture has been developed for the execution of highly optimized compiled Prolog code the underlying computational concept is just as applicable for interpreter based Prolog systems. Other design criteria were: low cost, modularity (i.e. the machine should be easily extendible), and a memory organization that is compatible with modern 32bit micro-processor systems.

Throughout the book it is assumed that the reader has had some prior exposure to Prolog and knows at least what unification is; however, any actual programming experience is not required.

In the remainder of this chapter I will briefly and informally discuss the foundation and history of logic programming. I will argue that the main parallel Prolog dialects fall short of the ideas advanced by the logic programming paradigm. This, and the required support of existing software, were the reasons why we chose not to develop another parallel Prolog dialect - a task better left to a language designer than to a computer architect.

Chapter 2 provides an overview of compilation techniques for high performance Prolog systems and defines the major Prolog data structures.

Chapter 3 gives an account of the parallel execution model and the synchronization requirements.

Chapter 4 shows how the occur-check problem can be solved for all practical purposes by distinguishing the context in which logical variables might occur. This chapter shows how work motivated by one problem can have far reaching ramifications. Originally the differentiation of variables according to their context was motivated by the desire to relax processor synchronization requirements. Later it was found that the new scheme also drastically reduced the bus contention and finally it was realized how this concept could be used to solve the occur-check problem.

Chapter 5 gives a complete specification of the abstract parallel Prolog machine. The internal data representation and the instruction set are specified. The reader who is not interested in the implementation details can safely skip this chapter.

Chapter 6 provides a qualitative and quantitative analysis of the parallel Prolog machine. It will be shown that the parallel machine is in all points superior to a comparable sequential machine.

Chapter 7 outlines the future research to be carried out and summarizes the contributions made by this thesis.

1.2 Historical Perspective and Foundations

Logic programming has its roots in the work on automated theorem proving and artificial intelligence. For well over fifty years there have been research efforts to construct automated deduction systems. One can even go back to Leibniz who dreamt of a 'calculator' which - by purely mechanical means - could derive answers to philosophical questions. However, the first serious work on automated deduction based on formal logic dates back to the work of Herbrand [He30] in 1930. This work was followed by others, and in 1965 Robinson [Ro65] introduced the resolution principle. The resolution principle is a sound and complete logical inference rule and represented an important breakthrough towards automated deduction systems. From an algorithmic point of view the resolution principle and its underlying unification operation are very well suited for an implementation on a computer. All that is required is the repeated application of the unification operation on a set of clauses that have been put into a standard form. One way to represent this standard form is the Gentzen Normal Form:

$$A_1, \ldots, A_n \leftarrow B_1, \ldots, B_m$$

where $A_1, \ldots, B_m$ are literals that can contain variables, atoms, and structures as arguments. The literals $A_1, \ldots, A_n$ are called positive literals with the commas denoting disjunction. The literals $B_1, \ldots, B_m$ are the negative literals of the clause and the commas denote conjunction. The informal semantics of $A_1, \ldots, A_n \leftarrow B_1, \ldots, B_n$ is "for each assignment of each variable, if $B_1 \wedge \ldots \wedge B_n$ is true, then one of the A_i ($0 < i \leq n$) must be true". Any formula in first order predicate logic can be very easily transformed into clausal form. If through repeated unification of a positive and negative literal the empty clause can be derived, then the

2

negation of the original statement is logically satisfiable, otherwise it is not (refutation process). A good introduction into the formal aspects of logic programming is [Ll84].

However, the early attempts to use Robinson's resolution principle and unification algorithm as the inference engine of a logic based computational model - despite their algorithmic simplicity - were not very successful. The main problem was the inability to subject the resolution principle to a natural control mechanism in order to restrict the search space and guide the resolution through the search space in a meaningful way. All the variants of the general resolution principle like hyperresolution, linear input resolution, etc. [CL73] were still not efficient enough to serve as a general purpose computational model. It was Kowalski [Ko74, Ko83] who recognized the procedural aspect of a restricted class of logical theories, namely Horn clause theories.

In order to appreciate the revolutionary idea that logic can in fact be used as a programming language let us informally review the notion of declarative versus procedural semantics in the context of Horn clause logic programming. A Horn clause has the following form:

$$A \leftarrow B_1, \ldots, B_n.$$

That is, Horn clauses have at most one positive literal, A, called the clause head (or consequent). The conjunction of the literals $B_1, \ldots, B_n$, the antecedent, is called the clause body. In the context of logic programming a Horn clause is also called a program clause. Of course, a program clause might have an empty body, i.e. it consists only of a clause head. A clause of this form is called a unit clause. A *logic program* is simply a finite collection of program clauses. According to this definition it is of course legitimate for there to be more than one clause with the same clause head literal. Intuitively one can regard program clauses as logical rules to solve a problem (goal) statement. Program clauses with the same head literal, called procedures, represent alternative ways of solving a problem statement, and unit clauses represent the 'facts' of the problem domain.

Let us consider the following goal statement (a goal statement is a clause with an empty consequent):

$$\leftarrow B(X, Y).$$

where X,Y denote variables. The question is whether this statement is a logical consequence of a given logic program P. If there exists an assignment, ψ, of values to the variables X and Y such that the goal statement B is a logical consequence of P then we call ψ a *correct answer substitution*. This definition of a *correct answer substitution* is one of the central ideas in logic programming and provides the basis of the *declarative semantics* of logic programming; if a goal statement is a logical consequence of a logic program then there exists an assignment of values to variables such that this assignment is a correct answer substitution. If no such assignment exists, then the goal statement is not a logical consequence of

3

the program. However, note that we haven't said anything about how to compute such correct answer substitutions. The declarative semantics of a logic program only provides a logical specification of the desired output from a program and a goal statement, and as such it is completely implementation independent.

Kowalski's idea was that Horn clauses of the form:

$$A \leftarrow B_1, B_2, \ldots, B_n \qquad n \geq 0$$

can - in addition to their declarative semantics - be given a procedural interpretation: to solve a goal statement A execute procedure A which consists of a conjunction of subgoals (subproblems) B_i; to solve the subproblems B_i execute the respective procedures B_i. When all subgoals have been solved, then the original goal A has been solved too. It is this procedural interpretation that distinguishes *logic programming* from *mechanical theorem proving*. It allows one to perform deductions from the logical specifications of computable functions in a goal directed manner. Note that this simple interpretation still does not say anything about the order in which the subgoals are executed or how clauses are selected for execution if there are several clauses that might be applicable to solve a particular goal.

In order to formalize the procedural interpretation one needs to specify the search and computation rules. The search rule determines the strategy in which clauses are tried to solve a given goal and the computation rule determines the order in which goals are selected. The procedural semantics of a logic programming is in general defined by the search and computation rule. There are, of course, many different possible search and computation rules each implementing a different semantics; however, it can be shown that there exists a search rule which gives rise to a procedural semantics which is identical to the declarative semantics. (It is immediately obvious that in order to implement the declarative semantics of logic the search rule must be independent of the computation rule. This is because the logical truth value of a conjunction of goals must be independent of their order.) Hence, under the right search rule the analog to the declarative *correct answer substitution* is the procedurally *computed answer substitution* and the two are identical; i.e. in the terminology of logic the procedural semantics is complete and sound. However, as we will see, actual programming languages based on the logic programming paradigm fall short of this mathematical ideal and sacrifice logical completeness for efficiency and ease of implementation. For a comprehensive discussion and formal mathematical treatment of the semantics of logic programming refer to [Ll84].

The first practical programming language based on Horn clause logic was Prolog (PROgramming in LOGic). Prolog was developed by Colmerauer and his group at the University of Marseille in 1972/73 [Co73]. However, to be able to implement the language efficiently the logical completeness of Horn clause logic was sacrificed - that is, the system might not find solutions implied by the declarative semantics. On the other hand, Prolog also contains many features that have no counterpart in the formal setting of Horn clause logic (e.g. dynamically deleting

4

and adding axioms to the program). A very good introduction into programming in Prolog and its features is [CM81].[1]

The execution rule of Prolog is very simple: the system executes all subgoals sequentially from left to right and considers candidate clauses sequentially in the textual order defined by the program. For a precise definition of the semantics of sequential Prolog, its shortcomings, and its relationship to Horn clause logic refer to [Ll84]. In this thesis we will be interested mainly in the efficient implementation of the semantics of sequential Prolog.

Since the declarative semantics does not impose any execution order on the goals or search order on the clauses, it is immediately obvious that logic programs *theoretically* provide much inherent parallelism. Three main forms of parallelism have been identified:

- *OR-parallelism* is the simultaneous invocation of all clauses capable of solving the current goal,

- *AND-parallelism* is the parallel execution of all subgoals within the current clause body,

- *unification-parallelism* is the concurrent unification of all arguments of a given goal and clause head literal.

Other forms of parallelism are merely restrictions of the above forms. However, the *unrestricted* use of AND/OR-parallelism leads to tremendous implementation problems and the associated overhead makes those schemes impratical. The main problem is the combinatorial explosion of processes and the creation of binding conflicts of variables.

Partly initiated by the "Fifth Generation Computer Systems" (FCGS) development project [Mo82] there have been considerable research efforts to define parallel Prolog dialects and corresponding massively parallel machines suitable for large scale parallel execution of Prolog programs [On85, Ta86]. The FCGS project is a large scale 10 year project initiated by the Japanese Ministry of Research and Technology and carried out in collaboration with major Japanese industrial companies. The research efforts are coordinated by the ICOT institute in Tokyo. The goals of the FCGS project have been widely publicized and will not be repeated here. However, it is an open question whether these goals can be met. The current approach of the FCGS project focuses on the use of massively parallel inference machines based on dataflow architectures [It85] and/or reduction machine architectures [On85]. These architectures consist of hundreds of thousands of processors on which special Prolog dialects can be executed in parallel. However, research in dataflow architectures in the last twenty years has failed to demonstrate their applicability for general purpose programming environments.

---

[1]In absence of an official language specification of Prolog this book also provides the de facto Prolog language standard.

In addition to the confounding architectural problems that exist, these machines require parallel Prolog dialects that allow one to express concurrency at the source level and whose semantic model is compatible with the parallel execution scheme. Standard sequential Prolog is not suitable for these proposed architectures because its search rule and semantic model does not allow for substantial amounts of AND/OR parallelism. It remains to be seen whether the semantic models of the parallel Prolog dialects under investigation are sound and strong enough to guarantee a wide spread user acceptance for general purpose logic programming.

1.3 Parallel Prolog Dialects

We will now briefly look at the major parallel Prolog dialects. The importance of parallel Prolog dialects lies not just in the performance gain over sequential Prolog but, more importantly, in their potential to implement the ideal, i.e. sound and complete, procedural semantics of logic programming. Unfortunately, it is especially the latter issue that the major parallel Prolog dialects do not address.

The following discussion must, of course, be incomplete since there are dozens of parallel Prolog dialects; however, most of these languages have never left the laboratory. The most widely investigated parallel Prolog dialects are Concurrent Prolog, Parlog, and Guarded Horn Clauses. All these dialects are parallel languages (i.e. they try to exploit AND/OR parallelism). This is not surprising since the FCGS' goal is to develop massively parallel computer systems. Space restrictions do not permit me to enter into a full discussion of all the subtle issues of each language's semantics. For a detailed review of parallel Prolog dialects the reader should refer to [Sy85, Gr87].

Concurrent Prolog: Concurrent Prolog was developed by E. Shapiro while he was a visting scientist at the ICOT [Sh83]. Concurrent Prolog is able to exploit both AND and OR parallelism. In order to overcome the synchronization problems associated with full AND and OR parallelism certain restrictions were imposed. To avoid binding conflicts, Concurrent Prolog provides a read-only operator. The read- only operator marks those variables within the clause body that can only be read. If a variable is a read-only variable, execution will automatically be suspended if the variable has not been bound by some other process. The suspension is in effect until some other process binds the respective variable, and then the suspended goal is reactivated. This requires the user to provide for each goal detailed information about the input/output behavior of the respective goal, a restriction not present in sequential Prolog and, in my opinion, contradictory to the declarative semantics of logic programming.

To implement OR parallelism Concurrent Prolog provides multiple environments in which to store conflicting bindings and a 'commit operator'. To understand the commit operator consider the following example:

$$A_1 \leftarrow G_{11}, G_{12}, G_{13} \mid B_{11}, B_{12}.$$
$$A_2 \leftarrow G_{21}, G_{22} \mid B_{21}, B_{22}, B_{23}.$$
$$A_3 \leftarrow G_{31} \mid B_{31}.$$

The subgoals G_{ij} are called guards, ' | ' is the commit operator, and the B's constitute the clause body proper. If a goal calls the above procedure all clauses $A_1, \ldots, A_3$ are executed in parallel; however, the clauses do not export bindings to the caller. When all guards have been successfully solved the commit operator is executed and all other clauses still running will be terminated. This process is semantically non-deterministic; that is, for the semantic model it is irrelevant which of the clauses 'commits' first. (This kind of semantic model is also called 'don't care non-determinism' since the system doesn't care which clause is selected as long as all the guards have been satisfied). When a clause has been committed and the other clauses have been terminated, the bindings of the chosen clause will then be exported to the caller. However, when a clause has been committed the other clauses can not be reactivated again. Hence, Concurrent Prolog does not provide any backtracking facilities. In the original language specification there were no restrictions on the guard goals. However, implementation problems and subtle semantic ambiguities have made it necessary to abandon the original approach and to restrict the guards to be system predicates that will not spawn new processes. To disallow user defined predicates as guards is of course a severe restriction. The restricted language is called 'Flat Concurrent Prolog'. A detailed account of the present day status of Concurrent Prolog is given in [Sh86].

PARLOG: The language Parlog was developed by Clark and Gregory at the Imperial College of Science and Technology [CG86]. Like Concurrent Prolog, Parlog also attempts to exploit AND and OR parallelism. It is somewhat similar to Concurrent Prolog in that it is a 'committed choice' language, i.e. it does not provide any backtracking facilities. As in Concurrent Prolog a procedure commits to a clause when all the guards of the respective clause have been satisfied. All other clauses running in OR parallel mode will then again be terminated. In order to avoid binding conflicts Parlog requires mode declarations for each procedure, thereby fixing the 'directionality' (i.e. the input/output behavior) of each clause. This is in contrast to Concurrent Prolog. In Concurrent Prolog it is the goals whose arguments are required to be in a certain mode. In Parlog the procedures have to be told which arguments are input and which are output arguments. Parlog also requires a global compile time analysis of the whole program to ascertain that no binding conflicts between OR parallel processes can result. Due to the complexity of the problem the compiler sometimes rejects programs as 'unsafe' (i.e. binding conflicts might result) even though the programs are semantically correct. A complete account of Parlog's design and implementations is given in [Gr87].

Guarded Horn Clauses: Guarded Horn Clauses is the latest development of a parallel Prolog dialect [Ue85]. It is also a 'committed choice language' like Concurrent Prolog and Parlog. It does not require any mode declarations or read-only annotations of goal variables. It is a very elegant language; however, its semantic model is not understood very well. Execution inefficiency has also made it necessary to restrict the guard goals to being system primitives. The restricted language is called 'Flat Guarded Horn Clauses'.

I will now briefly criticize the design of these parallel Prolog dialects. This is in no way meant to be a negative critique of the past and present research efforts towards defining a parallel Prolog language. However, it will clarify why the decision was made to base the Prolog machine presented in this thesis on sequential Prolog. All the major parallel Prolog languages are 'comitted choice languages' and do not support backtracking. Therefore, they can provide only one solution to any given problem. In order to find more than one solution special set constructor predicates must be used that generate a stream of solutions. The lack of backtracking facilities to implement 'don't know non-determinism' - an execution model where the system can not commit itself to an initial choice but might backtrack later on to revise that decision - makes it difficult to implement deductive databases. This might be a reason why parallel Prolog languages have not gained any widespread acceptance as programming languages for AI applications. For the most part they have been used to show how *system programming* can be done within the framework of logic programming.

The parallel Prolog languages overcome some of the problems of sequential Prolog; however, they also introduce new ones. While sequential Prolog has many logical deficencies, at least they are well understood, whereas the semantics of parallel Prolog languages is understood very little. It can be safely said that they have failed to capture the declarative and procedural semantics of standard logic programming. Shapiro himself admits that Concurrent Prolog is an ad hoc design to investigate the possibilities of parallel logic programming [Sh86] rather than a sound semantic model of parallel logic programming. In the case of languages like Guarded Horn Clauses and Parlog it might be very difficult to prove them deadlock free.

While it is true that the applicability of parallel Prolog languages to certain applications has been extensively studied, they also failed to gain any wide spread acceptance as viable programming languages outside the research centers where they were developed. Standard sequential Prolog, on the other hand, has found a large following and is now a viable alternative to LISP. Substantial amounts of software have already been written in sequential Prolog. Hence, there is a great demand for high performance Prolog machines. As far as performance is concerned the parallel Prolog dialects have so far failed to out-perform sequential Prolog for *general* applications. Even on special architectures under development at ICOT it has not been convincingly demonstrated that those systems will be any faster than high performance workstations for sequential Prolog. A description of the various approaches taken by the Japanese machine designers can be found in [On85, Ta86, It85]. Unfortunately the published accounts of the parallel machine architectures lack the detail needed to assess their merit.

In my opinion it is more important to provide a cleaner semantical model of sequential Prolog than to try to define yet another parallel Prolog dialect. The work of Naish [Na86] is an important example of an attempt to restore the logical completeness and the semantics of Horn clause logic within the framework of Prolog. I also believe it is very important to extend the language towards type concepts (i.e. many sorted logics) and to be able to express equational theories within the languages [AS87, Sm86/1, Sm86/2]. In my opinion it is these concepts that would make Prolog a very powerful language for AI applications rather than indiscriminate parallelism.

2 Compilation of Sequential Prolog

2.1 Sequential Prolog

As mentioned, before the language Prolog was developed by Colmerauer in Marseille in 1972/73 [Co73]. Since Prolog was meant to be a practical tool for logic programming, efficiency of language execution was a primary objective. The syntactical structure of Prolog programs is based on Horn clause logic, i.e. Prolog programs consist of a collection of clauses, as described in Chapter 1. In order to provide reasonable efficiency Prolog employs a particularly simple search and computation rule. The search rule of Prolog explores the search tree depth first; that is, Prolog considers sequentially one clause after another starting with the topmost clause. Whenever the system cannot solve the current goal it will backtrack to consider another clause. Within a clause the goals of the clause body are executed left to right. That is, all the subgoals of a goal statement are executed sequentially. This strategy of a *fixed order depth first* search rule and a left to right computation rule greatly simplifies the needed runtime structures. As a matter of fact, this execution model can easily be mapped onto a stack based architecture. Unfortunately, however, this search/computation rule does *not* give rise to a procedural semantics that is identical to the declarative semantics, i.e. the procedural semantics of Prolog is incomplete with respect to the declarative reading. The practical consequence is that a Prolog program might fail to find a solution even though the program is logically correct - a situation every Prolog programmer has encountered at least once. Hence, in writing Prolog programs the programmer has to keep Prolog's procedural semantics in mind and cannot program in a declarative style.

A further problem with Prolog is that the unification operation is usually implemented without occur-check. This means that a variable X can be unified with a term[1] even if variable X occurs within the term t. For example it is possible to unify X with t(X), resulting in the cyclic structure $t(t(t(t(\dots))))$. Plaisted [Pl84] showed how it is possible to write formally correct Prolog programs using first-order predicate calculus semantics and yet derive nonsense results such as $3 < 2$. One way to deal with this problem is to turn a bug into a feature. Colmerauer [Co82] developed a formal semantics of Prolog using infinite trees; this allows terms with loops to be regarded as infinite trees. However, this is not the standard semantics any longer, and there are applications that require the semantic model of first-order predicate calculus, i.e. unification with occur-check. Consider for example the use of difference lists to concatenate two lists in constant time.[2]. This

---

[1] A term is defined recursively as follows: a variable is a term, a constant is a term, and if f is a n-ary function and $t_1, \dots, t_n$ are terms then $f(t_1, \dots, t_n)$ is a term.

[2] Difference-lists/structures are an important concept in Prolog programming since they allow many operations to be carried out in constant time (rather than time proportional to the size of the list/structure) [Sh86/3] However, unlike similar operations provided in other languages, e.g. *rplcad* in Lisp, the use of difference-structures does not depend on destructive assignment.

can be achieved through a single unit clause:

$$\text{concat(X-Y, Y-Z, X-Z)}.$$

When this clause is called by the goal concat([1,2|X]-X, [3,4]-[ ], U-Z) the goal will succeed and U will be correctly instantiated to [1,2,3,4] (Z=[ ]). However, in a Prolog system without occur-check the goal concat(X-X, Y-Y, [a|Z]-Z) will also succeed. This is clearly wrong since in difference list notation X-X and Y-Y just denote the empty list, [ ]. But the concatenation of two empty lists cannot result in a list with the constant 'a' as its first element.

It should be obvious why the occur-check is rarely implemented. Without occur-check a variable and a structure can be unified in constant time. With occur-check unification is proportional to the size of the structure because every time a variable is bound to a structure, the structure has to be traversed to detect whether the variable is already part of the structure. Since through repeated unification structures can be made to grow exponentially simple unification with occur-check has exponential complexity. However, there are more sophisticated unification algorithms *with* occur-check that have quadratic over even linear complexity [PW78, MM82][3], but these algorithms require the structures to be unified to be in a special format. In practice this means that the structures have to be pre-processed to eliminate common subexpressions and to indicate data dependencies. This works as long as one deals with statically known structures; however, in Prolog structures are usually generated dynamically in a non-deterministic way, and pre-processing the structures for unification might involve as much overhead as it saves during the actual unification. Nonetheless, pre-processing of Prolog programs with a subsequent program transformation is an important optimization to simplify run-time unification, but it does not solve the occur-check problem for *dynamically* generated structures and/or data dependencies. This idea of simplifying the unification by a pre-processing step is actually one of the ideas behind the compilation of Prolog programs [Ku86]. In chapter 4 we will see how this idea can be developed further to take dynamically generated data dependencies into account.

The first Prolog systems were interpreter based systems: The Prolog program was regarded as a passive data structure which was interpreted according to Prolog's depth first search rule and right-to-left computation rule. Even though Prolog's procedural semantics was recognized early on, it was not clear how to apply implementation methods of other programming languages to the implementation of Prolog. Unlike more conventional programming languages Prolog systems must be able to backtrack to an earlier computational state. This of course requires that earlier machine states must still be accessible or that they can be reconstructed

---

[3]These papers also provide a good introduction to the subject of unification from an algorithmic/mathematical point of view.

from the present machine state. It was not clear how one could reconcile these requirements with an efficient implementation.

It took about five years after the inception of Prolog for the first Prolog compiler to come into existence [Wa77/1, Wa77/2]. With hindsight and our much better understanding of the many issues associated with the Prolog runtime environment it has become much easier to envision an abstract Prolog compiler. Studies are now under way to formalize the design of Prolog compilers rather than treating it as a black art [Ku86].

In a compiler based system the Prolog program is not a passive data structure any longer, rather all the operations previously carried out by the interpreter have been compiled into the Prolog program. One can view the step from an interpreted to a compiled Prolog system as the merging of an interpreter and a given Prolog program. An interpreter must of course be able to interpret any Prolog program. However, when merged with a particular Prolog program the interpreter can be optimized so that it will only be able to interpret the program at hand. This optimization defines a set of operations necessary to implement a particular Prolog program. This, of course, is not how practical compilers proceed; however, this view helps us to understand the necessary operations which form the basis of compiled Prolog.

One problem is that not all of the Prolog program is known at compile time since Prolog allows for the dynamic modification of its procedures. There are two possible solutions to this problem:

1. the compiler does not discard the whole symbol table after compilation and allows for the re-compilation/linking of dynamically modified procedures. This is the standard situation for systems that allow incremental compilation.

2. dynamically modifiable procedures will not be compiled at all but only interpreted. This makes it necessary to explicitly declare procedures as modifiable.

Since the focus of this work is the design of a Prolog machine we will not enter into a detailed discussion on how to compile Prolog programs but rather concentrate on the abstract machine operations and the data structures that facilitate the compilation of Prolog.

2.2 General Principles of Prolog Compiler Construction

What makes the design of a Prolog compiler so difficult is the necessity of identifying a set of low level operations in which to express the language semantics. To write a Prolog compiler is to first of all define an abstract machine with appropriate data structures and machine instructions. For example, we have to decide what information goes into a choice point, how to implement the unification operation and how to represent the Prolog search tree. In addition to the unification code for the clause head a good compiler generates in-line code for the clause selection and backtracking operation. And, of course, a compiler must also generate code for the memory management of the Prolog system, as well as in-line code for procedure calls. Let us assume we have the following clause:

$$h(\dots) \leftarrow s1(\dots), s2(\dots).$$

The compiled code for this clause will have to perform roughly the following actions:

- allocate environment,
  unify $h(\dots)$ with the calling goal,
- initialize argument registers for s1,
- call s1,
- initialize argument registers for s2,
- call s2,
- deallocate environment,
- return from clause.

All the actions marked with a • (i.e. the actual unification) are operations that can be considered overhead[4] since they don't contribute to the solution of the problem at hand. Later we will see how these actions can be optimized, which might also mean performing the actions in a different order than given in this example. Reducing the overhead associated with the execution of Prolog programs is at the heart of this thesis. If there is more than one clause with the same clause head literal control instructions are also needed to determine which clause to select for execution.

It was D.H.D Warren who incorporated all these operations into a very powerful abstract Prolog instruction set [Wa83]. The Warren instruction set has since become a de facto standard for high performance compiled Prolog systems. However, there are many other abstract Prolog instruction sets [Cl85, Ka86]. They are all based on the same principles and usually differ only in particular implementation details. Once one has understood the basic compilation principles there are many equally viable alternatives to implement these principles. Our own instruction set is based on the ideas put forward by David Warren but also differs in many important aspects. However, before we can delve into the specifics of the

---

[4]The notion of 'overhead' is used here to denote operations that do not affect the user data as given by the source code of the Prolog program. The user is only interested in the computation of the correct answer substitution according to the underlying procedural semantics. The low-level operations that implement the procedural semantics are transparent to the user and from his point of view are considered overhead. It is only the actual unification step that directly involves the user defined data structures.

complete Prolog instruction set it is necessary to understand the underlying data structures and their implementation.

We will now look at some of the issues involved in the compilation of Prolog programs. For many of the details left unanswered in the remainder of this chapter the reader is referred to chapters 4 and 5.

2.2.1 Data Typing

Due to the non-deterministic nature of Prolog the goal arguments are unknown at compile time. For example, consider the following Prolog fragment:

$$\ldots, g(X), \ldots$$

$$g(a).$$

The system must be able to determine at runtime, when $g(X)$ and $g(a)$ are unified, what the argument X refers to. The following cases can occur:

- X refers to an uninstantiated variable, in which case X will be assigned the constant 'a' and unification succeeds.[5]

- X itself refers to a constant 'a', in which case unification of $g(X)$ and $g(a)$ succeeds.

- X refers to some term which is neither an unbound variable nor the constant 'a', in which case unification fails.

This requires that Prolog systems must be able to determine the data type of the terms to be unified at runtime. The common technique is data type 'tagging'; that is, every Prolog term carries a tag to indicate its type. The basic data types in Prolog are: atom, integer, structure, list, and variable.[6]

A special situation arises when one variable refers to some other unbound variable as in the following example:

$$\text{test} :\text{-} g(X), \ldots$$

$$g(U) :\text{-} \ldots$$

---

[5] i.e. X becomes bound to 'a'.

[6] We will generically refer to atoms and integers as constants. The empty list is internally usually treated as a special constant with tag 'NIL'. Different Prolog dialects often also provide floating point data types.

In this case U refers to variable X, which at the time $g(U)$ is called is still unbound. Internally this fact is expressed as a special tag, 'REF' and a pointer to X. However, this tag does not constitute a user visible data type. It simply means that in order to find the data type (and/or value) of U the system has to look at X.[7]

2.2.2 Runtime Memory Management

Most modern Prolog implementations operate with three stacks:

Local Stack: The stack on which environments and choice points will be allocated,

Global Stack: The stack on which all structured data objects (e.g. lists) will be stored.

Trail Stack: The stack on which the address of variables will be pushed that have to be reset to UNBOUND when backtracking occurs. Consider the following clauses:

$$
\begin{aligned}
h(X,Y) &\leftarrow s1(U), s2(U, X, Y).\\
s1(a) &\leftarrow \ldots\\
s1(Z) &\leftarrow \ldots
\end{aligned}
$$

When s1 is called the first time the variable U, at that point an unbound variable, will be instantiated to the constant 'a'. However, when backtracking occurs the variable U needs to be reset to its original unbound state, so that the variable Z can be bound to an unbound variable as required by the semantics of Prolog. Hence, we need to be able to remember which variables need to be reset when backtracking happens.

Environments are vectors of consecutive memory cells which are allocated on the local stack. For every clause with more than one goal in the clause body an environment needs to be created (clauses with less than two subgoals do not need an environment). An environment contains the variables that occur in the clause and two control words. The environment of a clause is basically a temporary (for the lifetime of the clause) local shared memory through which the subgoals of the clause communicate their partial results to the following subgoals in the clause body. This explains why clauses with less than two subgoals do not need an environment - there is simply no need to pass partial results to other subgoals within the same clause. Variables that only serve to transfer arguments of the clause head to the first subgoal do not need to be stored in an environment but can be kept in registers; they are therefore called temporary variables. The two control words that are saved in the current environment are the return address,

---

[7]technically this is called 'dereferencing'

Continst, and a pointer to the previous environment. When the current clause is left after the last goal in the clause body has been solved, the clause environment can be discarded. The stack space can only be freed provided there are no untried alternative solutions for previous goals in the current clause. As an example, let us assume the current clause has the form:

$$h(X,Y) \leftarrow s1(X,U), s2(U,Y), s3(X).$$

This clause has three variables (X, Y, and U) in its environment. If there are untried alternative clauses for the goal s2 (i.e. s2 has created a backtrack point on top of the current environment) the current environment cannot be released after all, since, upon backtracking, s2 (and later s3) will still need to access the environment. The consequence is that environments can only be taken off the stack if no choice points appear after the current environment.

It is important to distinguish between logically discarding an environment and physically deallocating an environment (i.e. freeing the stack space). When a clause is left the environment will always be logically discarded, i.e. the environment pointer will be reset to point to the previous environment on the stack, which will now be the current environment (similiar to block structured languages such as Pascal). However, the stack space cannot always be released too. In this respect Prolog is very different from other languages. This is because of its nondeterministic nature. Only when all the goals within the current clause have terminated deterministically (or have been made deterministic by a CUT operation) can the environment be physically taken off the stack.

In order to be able to discard environments it is necessary to adhere to a strict order for binding variables. When two variables are bound, the binding must always be in the direction from the top to the bottom of the environment stack. The first Prolog interpreter violated this condition and could therefore only physically deallocate environments upon backtracking.

Variables that occur within structured data objects must be allocated on a different stack (commonly called the global stack or heap) since structures have a potentially longer lifetime than environments. Consider the following example:

$$\ldots, g(X), \ldots$$

$$g(f(U,V,W)) :- s(U), t(W).$$
$$s(a).$$
$$t(a).$$

The procedure g is deterministic and therefore its environment can be physically deallocated upon exit. However, the structure f(U,V,W) has been 'exported' to

16

the caller. This requires that all components of the structure must remain accessible; hence, the variables U,V, and W must be allocated on the global stack as part of the structure f. The stack on which structures are created can only be contracted upon backtracking. Since all objects on the global stack have a potentially longer lifetime than variables on the local stack, it is not permitted to have any pointers from the global stack to the local stack, as this might give rise to dangling references.

Choice Points: A choice point needs to be created whenever there is more than one clause in the procedure that might potentially unify with the current goal. Choice points and environments are logically independent; however, early implementations did not make this distinction. In those implementations the clause environment also contained the necessary information to handle backtracking. It is obvious that this creates overhead for purely deterministic goals.

The choice point (or backtrack point) contains all the information necessary to reset the Prolog machine to a previous state should a FAIL condition arise (i.e. when unfication between a goal and a clause header fails). To understand what information must be saved, consider the following example:

$$h(X,Y) \leftarrow s1(U,X), \quad s2(Y,V), \quad s3(X,Y,U,V).$$

$$\qquad\qquad\qquad\qquad\quad \uparrow \qquad\quad \uparrow$$

$$\qquad\qquad\qquad\qquad\quad \text{current} \quad \text{Continst}$$

$$\qquad\qquad\qquad\qquad\quad \text{goal}$$

$$\qquad\qquad\qquad s2(\ldots) \leftarrow \ldots$$

$$\text{Nextclause} \rightarrow \quad s2(\ldots) \leftarrow \ldots$$

$$\qquad\qquad\qquad s2(\ldots) \leftarrow \ldots$$

Let us make the following assumptions: the current goal is s2, there are untried alternatives for s1 (i.e. s1 has itself created a choice point), and all three clauses in procedure s2 can potentially match the current goal. When procedure s2 is entered a choice point is created, and the following information must be saved:

Currenv: A pointer to the environment of the calling goal. When backtracking to s2 occurs at some later time the system needs to know the context in which the calling goal had occurred. In this case the environment pointer points to the environment of clause h(X,Y) with the variables X,Y,U, V stored in it.

Continst: The address to return to when s2 has been successfully completed. The return address is being saved twice - in the choice point, as well as in the environments for the clauses of procedure s2.[8] When s2 is called for the first time the return address is just the next word following the call instruction; however,

---

[8]This seems redundant; however, note that not all clauses that have a choice point associated with them also require an environment. And, the other way around, clauses which require an environment might not be part of a choice point. To cover all situations the return address needs to be saved twice in order to avoid having to figure out which situation we are currently in.

17

when backtracking occurs we will not go back to the point of call but rather go immediately to the next clause to be considered for solving s2. At this point the original return address would not have been known any longer had it not been saved in the choice point.

Nextclause: The address of the next clause to be tried within a procedure.

Lastchpnt: The address of the previous choice point on the local stack. Should no attempt avail to solve the current goal we must backtrack to the previous choice point. Since, upon creating a new choice point, the Lastchpnt register will be overwritten, its value must be saved in the new choice point.

TPOS, GPOS: The stack pointers for the trail stack and the global stack. When backtracking occurs these stack pointers need to be reset to their previous value, thus discarding whatever has been put on the stack since the choice point was created. The *top-of-local-stack* pointer does not need to be saved since the local stack will automatically be contracted to the position of the choice point when backtracking occurs.

Additionally, all arguments of the current goal need to be saved, either explicitly or implicitly by just saving a pointer to the argument block.

Upon encountering a *FAIL* condition the system will access the last choice point and restore all registers with the values stored in the choice point. All variables saved on the trail stack between the current *top-of-trail-stack* and the old *top-of-trail-stack* stored in the choice point will be reset to an unbound state.[9] Execution will then proceed at the address stored in *Nextclause.*

A paper by Bruynooghe [Br82] provides a very good overview of memory management schemes of Prolog implementations.

2.2.3 Compilation of the Unification Algorithm

Most existing unification algorithms deal with the problem of unifying two (or more) unknown terms. However, when unifying a goal with a clause head the structure of the header is, of course, known. Consider the following case in which a goal and clause head have to be unified:

$$
\begin{array}{ll}
\text{goal} & \text{h}(\ X,\ Y,\ Z\ ) \\
\text{clause head} & \text{h}(\ U,\ [V|W],\ [a]\ ).
\end{array}
$$

(The notation is based on the Prolog syntax described in [CM81]). The structure of the goal arguments is not known at compile time since the variables might

---

[9]It is immediately obvious that only those variables that lie before the current choice point need to be trailed. Anything that was created on the local or global stack after the current choice point was created will automatically be discarded upon backtracking and does not explicitly need to be reset. Hence, when a variable becomes bound we need to check the variable's relative position with respect to the current choice point. If the variable lies above the current choice point or above the old *top-of-global-stack* stored in the choice point, then the variable will not have to be trailed. (see Chapter 5 for details).

18

become instantiated to just about anything at run time. The structure of the header, on the other hand, has been completely specified when the program was created. (The first argument is an unbound variable, the second argument is a list, the list header as well as the list tail are unbound variables, and the last argument is a list with one element, the constant 'a'). Given this structural information we can generate code for a unification algorithm that can only unify terms that have the very same structure as the clause head, but does it very efficiently. In principle, what is being done when Prolog programs are compiled, is that code for a highly specialized unification algorithm is being generated for every clause head. However, the unification code to be executed does not only depend on the structure of the clause head but also on the parameters of the calling goal.

Consider the following goal and clause head literal to be unified:

$$
\begin{array}{ll}
\text{goal} & g(X) \\
\text{clause head} & g(\ s(a)\ ) \leftarrow \ldots
\end{array}
$$

If the actual parameter X is still an uninstantiated variable, the structure s(a) will have to be created, and X will be bound to this newly created structure. On the other hand, if X has already been bound previously to some structure, the structure s(a) will be matched against this already existing structure and no new structure s(a) will be created.

2.2.4 Clause Indexing

Prolog procedures generally are not deterministic, i.e. they consist of more than one clause that might be applicable to solve a given goal. However, for a particular goal instance there is often only one clause that can possibly be unified with the calling goal. Consider the following program to concatenate two lists:

?- append([a,b,c], [d,e], R).

C1   append([ ], X, X).
C2   append([H|T], X, [H|T2]) ← append(T, X, T2).

In this particular example the clause C1 of the procedure *append* can immediately be discarded as a candidate to solve the current goal because the empty list, [ ], is not unifiable with the goal argument [a,b,c]. Only the clause head of clause C2 unifies with the current goal, thus making the procedure *append* in this example deterministic. Hence it is desirable to quickly filter out those clauses that cannot possibly unify with a particular goal instance, thereby saving unnecessary unification attempts and backtrack operations (i.e. restricting the search space). This can be done in several ways. For example, one can encode the data types of all the arguments of the current goal into a bit pattern and compare this pattern with the type pattern of the clauses of the called procedure [Wi84]. Another alternative is to use only the type information of one particular goal argument to hash into the set of clauses whose corresponding argument is of the same type. If the type is an atom or integer we can then hash again using the argument value as a hash key, thereby restricting the candidate clause set even further.

2.2.5 Tail Recursion Optimization and Mode Declarations

Tail recursion optimization is a very important concept for high performance Prolog systems. Tail recursion optimization for Prolog implementations were first introduced by Bruynooghe and Warren [Br82],[Wa80]. The central idea is to discard environments prior to the last call. Consider the following example:

$$t(X) \leftarrow s1(X,U), s2(U,V), s3(V).$$

In an ordinary implementation procedure s3 would, after having been completed successfully, return to the parent clause to discard the environment. However, since there are no other goals in the current clause which might need the environment the environment can be discarded right away before s3 is called. If we assume that the stack space can actually be freed, tail recursion optimization will save considerable stack space because procedure s3 can reuse the just freed stack space. This is especially important for recursive procedures with deep recursion depth. The name 'tail recursion optimization' is actually a misnomer since the concept applies to every last call of a clause body, not just recursive calls. However, the scheme yields the greatest savings for recursive calls and is also known under this name in other programming languages. For subtle problems introduced by the tail recursion optimization see chapters 3 and 5.

Mode declarations are also an important optimization for Prolog systems. Generally Prolog does not require the user to specify which parameters of a procedure are input or output parameters. The program *append* can either be called as append([1,2],[3],X) to concatenate two lists or as append(Y,[3],[1,2,3]) to find the list which concatenated with [3] will result in the list [1,2,3]. However, often it is a priori known that a certain procedure will only be used a certain way. By telling the system what parameters will be input or output parameters the compiler can perform important optimizations. Especially the presented parallel Prolog machine can greatly benefit from mode declarations. The argument that mode declarations are too restrictive can be countered with the fact that very often mode declarations are already implicitly provided because most built-in predicates require their parameters to be instantiated in a certain way. This information can be used to automatically deduce mode declarations for higher level user predicates.

3 Pipelined Execution of Sequential Prolog

3.1 Introduction

In this chapter a pipelined architecture of tightly coupled processors is presented that allows for the parallel execution of several independent unification operations. It will be demonstrated how even fully deterministic Prolog programs with no apparent inherent parallelism can be effectively mapped onto a processor pipeline. An important aspect of the execution model will be that it is possible to drastically reduce the effects of implementation dependent overhead functions, such as allocating/deallocating stack space, creating choice points, parameter passing, address calculation, etc. (about half the execution time of a typical Prolog program is wasted performing such overhead operations).

Pipelining the execution flow of a program is of course nothing new. There is probably not a single field within the realm of information processing where it has not been successfully employed. Pipelining principles can be applied at various levels:

- *Pipelining at the micro-instruction level.*
  While one micro-instruction is executing, the next micro-instruction will be fetched. *Requirements:* independent micro-instruction sequencer and execution unit.

- *Pipelining at the machine(macro)-instruction level.*
  Assembler instructions are independently fetched, decoded, and executed. *Requirements:* autonomous fetch, decode, and execution units (possibly several independent execution units).

- *Pipelining of blocks of code.*
  Requirements: a pipeline of tightly coupled independent processors.

It should be obvious that those concepts are orthogonal. Whereas nowadays pipelining at the first two levels is supported by every micro-processor, it is not so clear how large blocks of code can be overlapped in a pipeline fashion. For fixed algorithms one can hope to structure the code in such a way as to be able to execute code chunks independently (i.e. explicitly extracting parallelism from a known algorithm/program). However, how can this be done for a general purpose environment, where the program is unknown and might not exhibit any explicit parallelism at the source level?

Before we take a closer look at the proposed system architecture and the intricacies of executing Prolog programs on it, it might be helpful to demonstrate the underlying principle. Consider the following fragment of a C program:

```
p( A, B, C);
    int   A,B,C;
{i = 5;
 j = A * B;
 q( C, j );}



main()
{ .
    .
p( 5, array[1,3], X );
    .

    .
}
```

A function *p* (with 3 scalar arguments) is called and in turn calls another function *q*. There seems to be no parallelism at the source level that could possibly be exploited; however, on the implementation level there is some parallelism even in this simple program.

Consider how this little program would typically be compiled:[11]

```
            load #5,A1
            .
            address
            calculation for
            array[1,3]
            .
            load array[1,3],A2
            load X,A3
            call p

       p:   allocate
            activation record
            i=5
            j=A1*A2
            load C,A1
            load j,A2
            call q
```

As can be seen from the above example, most operations are implementation dependent overhead that is not visible at the source level. It really does not

---

[11]We shall assume that the actual parameters are being passed in special argument registers, A1,...,An.

matter whether the parameters are passed on the stack or in registers, whether call-by-value or call-by-reference is employed etc.. It is my premise that every concrete implementation of an abstract entity such as a programming language will introduce some overhead. However, it is exactly these overhead operations that can often be executed concurrently. For example, why should the function p not allocate its environment, and maybe even perform some local computation, while the actual arguments are being set up? The function p can also start using those arguments that are already known; why should a procedure always have to wait until *all* its parameters have been determined? Of course, realization of such a concept requires a multiprocessor environment with appropriate synchronization primitives. Given such a system the example above could be executed as follows:

Processor 1		Processor 2
call p		
load #5,A1	p:	allocate
.		activation record
address		call q
calculation for		i=5
array[1,3]		j=A1 *...
.		*delay until A2 is available*
load array[1,3],A2		A2
load X,A3		load j,A2
stop		load A3,A1
		stop

Instead of waiting until all the arguments have been set up the function call is issued right away, thereby enabling the next processor to start execution of the called procedure. Execution can proceed until an argument is needed that has not yet been provided by the caller; execution will automatically delay until the required argument becomes available.

We will now look at an architecture capable of supporting this kind of parallelism and study in some detail how Prolog programs can be mapped onto such a pipeline architecture. However, the little example above has demonstrated that the general principle should be applicable to other programming languages as well (especially functional languages).

3.2 A Pipelined Architecture for Prolog

We have just seen, albeit in a very abstract way, how function calls in C can be pipelined on a multi-processor system. The same idea should be applicable for Prolog programs. Operationally the execution of Prolog programs consists solely of procedure calls, with unification as the underlying parameter passing mechanism. However, due to the non-determinism of Prolog programs the procedure calls generally involve more computation than simple C function calls. In the remainder of this chapter I will demonstrate how Prolog procedure calls can be mapped onto a multi-processor environment. Before we can discuss the execution model, we have to take a look at the global architecture that is to support the execution model.

Looking at the parallel execution model of the C function call given above, a few questions immediately come to mind:

1. Where are the argument registers located?

2. How is the synchronization accomplished (e.g. the automatic insertion of wait states when an argument is not available)?

3. How is the stack pointer shared between the processors? How is the access to the stack pointer synchronized?

4. What is the topology of the multi-processor system?

Of course, there are many ways to implement this execution model. For example, we could put all the argument registers into a shared memory section and sychronize access to them through software monitors. For a fine grained operation such as a function call this would introduce an unacceptable overhead. However, a procedure call, be it in C or Prolog, establishes a very local and well defined communication channel between caller and callee. The idea is to keep caller and callee on adjacent processors and to provide a very fast communication link between the two processors. To support a sequence of procedure calls, i.e. A calls B calls C calls D, we can extend this basic pipelining principle to include more pipeline stages.

The hardware structure of the proposed system is shown in Figure 3-1. It has been designed to work as a co-processor to a more conventional UNIX based workstation. This is a very important constraint. It requires that the co-processor be architecturally compatible with the host computer. For example, in order to efficiently communicate with the host computer the co-processor should have the same memory word width as the host machine. This in turn predicates that the data type tags must be incorporated in the standard word width (see Chapter 5). However, a co-processor solution has convincing advantages: a co-processor is less complex, and thereby less expensive, than a stand alone machine, and the co-processor can be integrated within a standard operating environment, such as UNIX, of the host machine. This gives the co-processor access to already existing software packages, user interfaces, and other programming languages. To port an environment such as UNIX to a new machine is a non-trivial task; especially when the architecture of the target machine is geared towards the execution of Prolog programs.

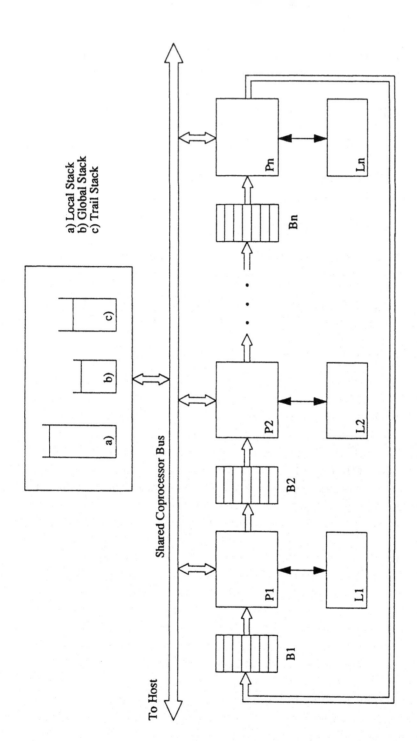

Figure 3-1: Global System Architecture

25

entry address of the next goal or procedure
Size (no. of arguments)
previous choice point
top-of-local-stack
top-of-global-stack
top-of-trail-stack
Nextclause (address of next clause to consider upon backtracking)
pointer to previous environment
continuation pointer
Arguments

Figure 3-2: Structure of a pipeline buffer block

The proposed co-processor architecture consists of a pipeline of unification processors, with every processor connected to its right neighbor. The last processor is connected with the first one, thereby creating a circular arrangement of processors. The processors are micro-programmable and have been designed to execute an abstract Prolog machine instruction set. All processors share access to a global system memory and may optionally possess a local memory of their own. A detailed acount on the design of the individual processors and possible system configurations is given in Chapter 6.

The shared memory contains all the typical Prolog data areas: namely the global stack for structured data objects, the local stack for the choice points and clause activation records (environments), and the trail stack for the recording of the variable bindings that need to be reset upon backtracking.

Between adjacent processors a pipeline buffer buffers and synchronizes the data exchange of the processors. Each pipeline buffer is organized as a ring buffer consisting of n fixed size memory blocks.[12] The structure of a pipeline buffer block is shown in Figure 3-2. Each buffer block consists of a collection of 9 control words and a set of registers that serve to pass the arguments of a goal to the called procedure. A typical configuration is to have a 256 word (1KByte) ring

---

[12]For the reason to have several pipeline buffer blocks see section 3.3.3 AND-Parallelism

buffer with 8 buffer blocks of 32 words each. Taking the 9 control words into account, this arbitrarily restricts the maximal number of arguments a goal can have to 23. However, for all practical purposes this number should be more than sufficient.[13] Statistics compiled from a large body of Prolog programs indicate that a goal has hardly ever more than 10 arguments. Generally the data exchange is uni-directional from left to right. All but the fields *Nextclause* and *Size* will be initialized by the left processor. Hardware semaphores built into the buffer guarantee that the right processor can only access buffer cells after the left processor has transfered data objects into the respective buffer cells. There are two pointers controlling the access to the buffer blocks of the ring buffer; one pointer belongs to the left processor, the other to the right processor.

As can be seen from Figure 3-2, all pointers necessary to access the global Prolog data areas in the shared memory will be passed around the pipeline. There are two basic reasons for this. The pointers have to be accessible to all processors in the pipeline. To place them in the shared memory would require every processor to access the global bus for obtaining the pointer. The shared bus, however, has the potential of becoming the one bottleneck in the system and, therefore, should only be used when absolutely necessary. It is much faster to pass the pointer around the pipeline. The second reason for passing the pointer from processor to processor is even more important. By explicitly sending one or the other pointer to the next processor, the compiler can generate code in such a way as to automatically control access to the various data areas in the shared memory and thus synchronize the processors. A detailed account of the processor-processor communication and their synchronization will be given later.

Even though the main purpose of the pipeline buffer is to serve as a communication buffer between processors, the remaining cells not used for the transfer of control information and arguments can be used by the processors as a local scratch pad.

3.3 Execution Model

The basic idea of the proposed parallel execution model for sequential Prolog is to execute the procedure calls in an overlapping pipeline fashion. The execution of a Prolog program is completely defined by a sequence of procedure calls, which is determined by the procedural semantics of Prolog. Viewing a procedure call as a basic operation, we will now develop the necessary mechanisms to pipeline these basic operations. The proposed architecture has been designed to execute compiled Prolog code, but the idea of treating procedure calls as basic operations to be pipelined can also be applied to interpreter based systems. However, generally only a compiler is able to take full advantage of a pipeline architecture,

---

[13]Of course, additional arguments can always be passed through the global shared memory. This, however, is much less eficient.

P_1		P_2		P_3		P_1
call h,NIL						
load X,A1*	h:	call g,s'				
load a,A2*		unify e,A1	g:	return		
load Y,A3*		unify Z,A2		wait		busy
load b,A4*		load Z,A1*		wait		busy
stop		load U,A2*		unify a,A1	s':	call s,...
		unify e,A3		unify a,A2		load A1*
		unify b,A4		stop		.
		stop				.
						stop

Figure 3-3: Execution Flow through the Pipeline

because the compiler can perform instruction scheduling and register allocation
to optimally match the pipeline architecture.

To understand how Prolog programs are being executed on the proposed architecture, consider the following fragment of a Prolog program:

$$?\text{-}h(X,a,Y,b).$$

$$C1 \quad h(e,Z,e,b) \leftarrow g(Z,U), s(\ldots), \ldots$$
$$C2 \quad g(a,a).$$

The actual progression through the pipeline can best be described by referring to
the code executed on the processors, as shown in Figure 3-3.[14] Assume processor
P_1 is to execute the current goal h(X,a,Y,b); further assume the pipeline consists
of 3 unification processors. Then execution proceeds as follows:

> Processor P_1 sends the entry address of clause C1 to processor
> P_2. Subsequently processor P_1 transfers one by one the arguments
> of the current goal to its right neighbor, processor P_2. Processor P_2
> picks up the entry address and attempts to unify the arguments of
> the current goal with the clause head of clause C1. However, before
> starting the actual unification operation it will send the entry address

---

[14]The instructions in Figure 3-3 are a simplified version of the actual instruction set and serve
only to demonstrate the execution principle. The argument registers have been denoted A1-An.
Register Ai* refers to the ith argument register of the right neighbor. Hence, the register which
the left processor refers to as Ai*, is being referred to by the right neighbor processor as Ai.

of its first subgoal to the next processor, P_3, in the pipeline. While processor P_2 is unifying the current goal, it will pass the arguments of the subgoal g(Z) to processor P_3 as they become available. Processor P_3 will proceed in exactly the same fashion.

The call instruction has two operands. It passes not only the entry address of the next procedure, but also a continuation pointer to the right neighbor. This pointer indicates which goal is to be executed next when the calling goal has been reduced to the empty clause (success continuation pointer). When a unit clause is reached, the parent goal's success continuation pointer is passed to the right neighbor, and the game starts all over again. Whenever an argument is not available yet, as can be seen in the case of processor P_3, the processor delays execution until the argument is provided by the left processor. This happens automatically and is directly controlled by the hardware semaphores which provide a low level data flow synchronization mechanism. When the last processor in the pipeline has been reached, the first processor is activated again.[15] The last processor writes the entry address of the next goal to be executed into the respective cell of the next free pipeline buffer block of the first processor. If the first processor is still busy, execution of the next goal will be delayed. As soon as the first processor becomes idle, it will examine the entry address cell of the next pipeline buffer block to find out whether there is another goal to be executed. If no new entry address has been provided yet, the processor will again automatically delay execution. The stop instruction terminates the current activity and waits for the next entry address.

It is also possible to have two or more Prolog programs executing concurrently on the pipeline. Since the pipeline buffer blocks contain all the state information of a particular Prolog process, it is possible to have different Prolog processes occupy different pipeline buffer blocks. Whenever a particular processor becomes idle it will just read the next pipeline buffer block and start execution of the goal contained therein.

To summarize, the arguments for a given goal can be established in parallel to the actual unification operation and the next goal to be solved can be processed concurrently with the previous goal. Of course, whenever a goal fails, all the processors to the right, having been invoked in anticipation of a successful unification, must be reset. At this point the flow through the pipeline becomes disrupted and the pipeline needs to be filled again. A schematic picture of the execution scheme is shown in Figure 3-4. The tuple notation $< T_i, P_j >$ represents an operation at time T_i on processor P_j. The shaded part in Figure 3-4b represents those times where the processors are idle. The idle time depends of course on the length of the pipeline and the average operation overlap. However, the idle time can be used to let another parallel process circulate through the pipeline. Hence, the proposed architecture is very well suited for the parallel execution of Prolog programs. Of

---

[15]Due to the circular pipeline structure it does not make sense to speak of a 'last' and 'first' processor; however, it helps to understand what happens when the pipeline becomes full.

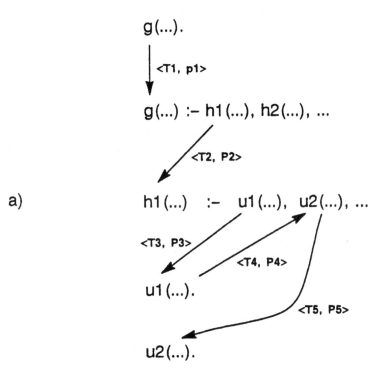

a)

$<T4,P4>$ represents the return from the unit clause u1(...)
and the initialization of the arguments of u2(...)

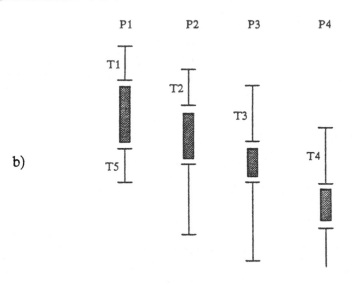

b)

Figure 3-4: Schematic display of pipelined execution of sequential Prolog

course, one can also use the 'shaded portion' to perform other operations, e.g. extensive type checking for Prolog dialects that incorporate a hierarchical sort system [Sm86/2].

3.3.1 Processor-Processor Communication and Synchronization

The previous section gave an account of the logical progression of a Prolog program through the pipeline of processors, without paying much attention to the actual communication and synchronization details. These issues shall now be dealt with. To understand the extent to which access to the shared memory must be controlled, three cases need to be distinguished:

- a processor might want to push (pop) data objects onto (off) one of the three Prolog stacks, thereby modifying the respective stack pointer (e.g. allocating activation records, creating choice points, creating global structures, and trailing/untrailing variable bindings);

- a processor might want to bind an already existing but still unbound variable;

- a processor might want to access existing and fully instantiated data objects.

The last case is uncritical because of the single assignment semantic of Prolog and does not require any special synchronization operations. Once a variable has been bound or a structure has been created, it cannot be changed any more.

Synchronization of Access to the Local Stack: It is obvious that two or more processors cannot simultaneously try to allocate an activation record on the same stack. The compiler guarantees that clause activation records and choice points will only be created in the fixed order required by the language semantics. Consider the following procedure:

$$h(\dots) \leftarrow s1(\dots), s2(\dots), \dots$$
$$h(\dots).$$

$$s1(\dots) \leftarrow t1(\dots), t2(\dots), \dots$$
$$s1(\dots).$$

The compiled code for the clause heads will roughly have to perform the following actions:

h: create choice point,
    allocate environment,
    call procedure s1,
    unify clause head with   s1: create choice point,
    the calling goal,   allocate environment,
    pass arguments of   call procedure t1,
    s1 to next processor,   unify clause head with
    stop   the calling goal s1(...),
                                         pass arguments of t1
                                         to the next processor,
                                         stop

The compiler generates the code in such a way that the call to the next goal will always occur after the choice point and environment of the current clause have been created. Hence, as soon as the next subgoal starts executing it can immediately proceed to create its own choice point and/or environment. Whenever a choice point or environment is created, the respective pointer is passed to the right neighbor. If no choice point or environment needs to be created, then the last choice point and current environment pointer that was received from the left neighbor will be passed on to the right. Hence all the pointers describing the status of the local stack (top of stack, last choice point, and current environment) are passed from processor to processor around the pipeline. This way whenever a processor obtains a pointer it is guaranteed that the pointer, or the object pointed to, will not change anymore.

However, implementation of the tail recursion optimization poses a problem. Tail recursion optimization implies that prior to invoking the last goal of the current clause the environment of this clause will be discarded. This can cause a problem in our execution model. Consider the following program:

$$
\begin{array}{lll}
\text{C1} & t(\dots) & \leftarrow \dots, h(X,Y,Z) \\
\text{C2} & h(U,V,W) & \leftarrow s1(), s2(\dots), \dots
\end{array}
$$

Invocation of procedure 'h' would proceed as follows:

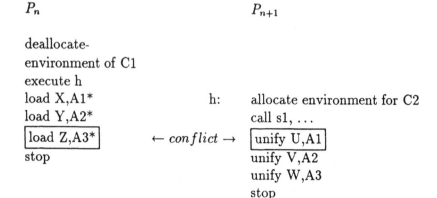

The old environment is deallocated before the procedure to solve the last goal is invoked. This is just the definition of tail recursion optimization; however, in our particular execution model it might still be necessary to access the old environment to initialize the argument registers. (In this case the values of the variables X, Y, and Z - which might be part of the just deallocated environment - have to be passed to the next processor). However, the next processor allocates a new environment (maybe re-using the just discarded storage space) and stores unification results in its environment, thereby potentially destroying information still needed. (In the example above, if the variable Z of clause C1 and variable U of clause C2 occupy the same relative position within the respective environments variable Z might be overwritten by U).

To solve this problem one can either give up tail recursion optimization - at least the part that recovers discarded stack space - or delay the invocation of the next procedure until the old environment can be safely overwritten. For the above example this would look as follows:

P_n P_{n+1}

load   X,A1*
load   Y,A2*
load   Z,A3*
deallocate
execute   h
stop   h: allocate
                                   unify U,A1

                                   ⋮

This will, of course, work; but we have compromised our execution model. In fact we have sequentialized the execution at this point and wouldn't even need to transfer control to the next processor. However, as we have seen in section 2.2.4., tail recursion optimization can not always free stack space, due to the semantic requirements of Prolog. On the other hand, even if stack space is freed it will not always be re-used immediately (remember not every clause requires an environment). Hence, execution needs only be sequentialized in those cases where the stack space of the old environment can actually be freed and where the called procedure wants to immediately allocate a new environment. This is accomplished by providing a special status flag as part of the current pipeline buffer block. If stack space on the local stack is freed by a deallocate operation this flag will be set. As long as this flag is set, the right neighbor processor is not able to execute an 'allocate' instruction. Of course, as long as no allocate instruction is executed, everything proceeds as usual. As soon as the left neighbor is done, the status flag will be reset and pending allocate instructions can be executed.

Synchronization of Access to the Global Stack: Access to the global stack is controlled through the explicit release of the respective stack pointers. Consider the following example:

$$?\text{-}h(f(b),Y,g(c,c)).$$

$$h(X,[1,2,3],Z) \leftarrow \ldots$$
$$h(\ldots).$$

Establishing the arguments of the given goal requires the creation of two structures on the global stack: f(b) and g(c,c). However, the called procedure also wants to create a structure on the global stack (the list [1,2,3]), yet the backtrack behavior of Prolog requires that the structures f(b) and g(c,c) occur before the list on the global stack. (Should the first clause of procedure h fail, the list [1,2,3] will have to be taken off the global stack again). This case is resolved dynamically at run time as follows:

call procedure h,	
create structure f(b),	h: create choice point,
pass pointer to f(b)	allocate environment,
to next processor,	call first subgoal,
pass Y to next processor,	unify X,A1
reserve space for g(c,c)	
on the global stack,	
release global stack pointer,	
construct g(c,c),	unify [1,2,3],A2
pass pointer to g(c,c)	unify Z,A3
to next processor,	stop
stop	

Since the unification of the list [1,2,3] with an unbound variable would result in the creation of the list, the respective unify instruction automatically delays execution until the global stack pointer becomes available (i.e. will not be used by the left neighbor any longer). It should be obvious that the pointer to the structure can only be passed to the right processor after the structure has been completely created.

The trail stack pointer is explicitly released in the same fashion. However, the trail stack pointer not only controls the access to the trail stack but also synchronizes the unification operations.

Synchronization to Avoid Binding Conflicts: So far we have not considered whether the concurrent unification of two goals might not result in binding conflicts. Consider the following example:

$$?\text{-}h(X,X,c,W), \ldots$$

C1	$h(Z,a,U,V) \leftarrow g(Z,U)$.
C2	$g(b,x)$.
C3	$g(a,x)$.

According to the execution model presented so far, the above example would be executed roughly as follows:

P_1	P_2		P_3
call h,...			
load X,A1*	h:	execute g	
load X,A2*		unify Z,A1	g: create choice point
load c,A3*		pass Z,A1*	return
load W,A4*		$\boxed{\text{unify a,A2}}$ $\leftarrow conflict \rightarrow$	$\boxed{\text{unify b,A1}}$
stop		unify U,A3*	$\vdots$
		pass U,A2*	
		unify V,A4	
		stop	

However, now it cannot be predicted who is going to "FAIL", processor P_2 or P_3. After the first argument of clause C1 has been unified (i.e. variable Z has been bound to variable X), this binding will be passed to the right processor, as the variable Z is the first argument of the goal g(Z). However, as soon as the processor working on clause C2 has possession of this argument, it will proceed with unifying the argument with the respective formal parameter of the clause

C2 (in this case binding variable X via the binding Z → X with the constant 'b'). Concurrently the left processor proceeds with unifying the remaining arguments of clause C1. Unfortunately, this process would result in assigning the constant 'a' to variable X. Due to this race condition in establishing the binding for variable X, correct program behavior cannot be guaranteed. The solution to this problem is to delay a processor's attempt to bind variables not in its own environment until its left hand neighbor has indicated that this can safely be done. This can easily be accomplished by controlling access to the trail stack. When a variable is being bound, it must be checked whether this binding needs to be recorded on the trail stack. Therefore any processor that might establish bindings of variables not in its own environment needs access to the trail stack. (The trail stack is accessed via the trail stack pointer). When it can be guaranteed that a processor will not bind nonlocal variables any longer, the trail stack pointer will be passed to the right neighbor, thus enabling the right processor to proceed in establishing nonlocal bindings. Whenever a processor finds a nonlocal variable as an argument and wants to assign a value to it, the processor must obtain the trail stack pointer first. However, access to the trail stack pointer is controlled through the hardware semaphores of the pipeline buffer. Hence, the right processor will automatically be delayed when trying to read the trail stack pointer from the buffer until the left processor has released the stack pointer. In the above example the processor unifying the goal h(X,X,c,W) with the clause head of clause C1 can release the trail stack pointer after unification of the second argument:

P_1		P_2		P_3
call h,...				
load X,A1*	h:	execute g		
load X,A2*		unify Z,A1	g:	create choice point
load c,A3*		pass Z,A1*		return
load W,A4*		unify a,A2		:
		release-tpos		
		unify U,A3		unify b,A1
		pass U,A2*		FAIL
		unify V,A4		
		stop		

Unification of the following arguments will only result in establishing bindings in its own environment. The right neighbor processor can now proceed to unify its arguments. Note that during the unification of the goal g(Z,U) the variable W (via the binding U → W) can now be safely bound, because through the release of the trail stack pointer the left processor has indicated that it will not attempt to change the status of the variable W any more. (Of course, it might bind other unbound variables to W).

Relaxing the Synchronization Requirements: These synchronization constraints can be relaxed by introducing special tags indicating that an unbound variable occurs only once within a given goal. Consider the following example:

$$?\text{-}h(X,Y,Z).$$

C1	$h(U,a,b) \leftarrow g(U).$
C2	$g(c).$

In this case the variable X can be bound to 'c' (via the binding $U \rightarrow X$), regardless of possible binding conflicts, as soon as the variable U has been passed to the processor unifying $g(U)$ and clause C2. The differentiation of variables according to the context in which they occur is a very important subject of this thesis. It will be studied in great detail in Chapter 4.

3.3.2 Implementation of Backtracking

As we have seen from the previous discussion, all the stack pointers, a pointer to the current environment, a pointer to the current choice point, a success continuation pointer (return address), and most important of all the goal arguments are being passed around the pipeline. When a processor has passed all this information to the next processor, this processor has the complete information of the current machine state (see Figure 3-2). Hence, the left pipeline buffer block contains exactly the information that a Prolog choice point ordinarily contains and can therefore be used as a choice point cache. Not only that, but choice points are created by default. One important concept is the distinction between 'shallow' and 'deep' backtracking. When the current goal does not change, and only different clauses within one procedure are being tried, we speak of 'shallow' backtracking. However, when all clauses that could match a given goal have been exhausted, backtracking to a previous procedure that has untried alternatives must take place; this is called 'deep' backtracking. As the definition implies, shallow backtracking does not require that the argument registers be reset. Whenever a procedure has several alternatives that might resolve the current goal, a choice point must be allocated. This is done in two steps. When the procedure is entered, space on the local stack will be reserved to accomodate the procedure's choice point. However, no choice point is actually created yet on the stack. As long as the current goal does not change we will work with the information contained in the left pipeline buffer. If a particular clause head of a nondeterministic procedure cannot be unified with the current goal, we will just reset those variables that might have become instantiated before the mismatch was detected and try another clause. No other registers need to be reset since the left pipeline buffer still contains the old (current) machine state. All changes to the machine state by the failed clause can only have affected the right neighbor which will be reset upon a fail anyway. If a clause head has been successfully unified with the current goal but there are still untried alternative clauses of the current procedure, then the machine state needs to be saved. This is because subsequent fails of other goals might make it necessary to backtrack to the current state ('deep' backtracking). To save the current machine state, the content of the left pipeline buffer block will be copied into the reserved block on the the local stack. Deep backtracking works the opposite way. The current procedure was not able to unify successfully with the current goal. We have to backtrack to a previous goal/procedure to find a different way through the Prolog search tree. A pointer to the last such alternative (i.e. the last choice point) is contained in the left pipeline block (entry 3 in Figure 3-2). The last choice point will then be copied from the local stack into the left pipeline buffer block, thereby re-establishing an old machine state. The present machine state can safely be overwritten since it led to a 'dead end' situation anyway.

3.3.3 AND-Parallelism

The presented architecture also supports a restricted form of AND- parallelism. Goals to be executed in parallel have to be data independent and must terminate deterministically. Data independent means that the goals to be executed in parallel do not share any unbound variables. Ground terms (i.e. atoms, integers, and structures that don't contain any unbound variables) can of course be shared. A typical example is the quicksort program:

$$
\begin{aligned}
&\text{qsort}([],[]).\\
&\text{qsort}([H|T],R) \quad \leftarrow \quad \text{split}(T,H,Sm,Lrg),\\
&\qquad\qquad\qquad\qquad\qquad \text{qsort}(Sm,R1),\\
&\qquad\qquad\qquad\qquad\qquad \text{qsort}(Lrg,R2),\\
&\qquad\qquad\qquad\qquad\qquad \text{append}(R1,[H|R2],R).
\end{aligned}
$$

Clearly the two recursive calls, qsort(Sm,R1) and qsort(Lrg,R2), can be executed in parallel. The recursive calls could have also been executed in parallel had the program been written in the widely used optimized form:

$$
\begin{aligned}
&\text{qsort}([],X,X).\\
&\text{qsort}([H|T],R,R0) \quad \leftarrow \quad \text{split}(T,H,Sm,Lrg),\\
&\qquad\qquad\qquad\qquad\qquad\quad \text{qsort}(Sm,R,[H|R1]),\\
&\qquad\qquad\qquad\qquad\qquad\quad \text{qsort}(Lrg,R,R1).
\end{aligned}
$$

In this case the involved goals share an unbound variable and hence are not data independent according to our definition. However, a simple global data flow analysis shows that the variable R1 will never become bound within the first

38

recursive call of qsort. Hence, it can not cause binding conflicts with bindings established in the second recursive call.

Detection of those goals that could be executed in parallel is accomplished through a global data flow analysis at compile time. However, the user can also explicitly indicate which goals can be executed in parallel. Parallel execution of data independent goals is implemented in the following way. Whenever two goals can be executed in parallel a fork operation is executed, switching both processes (goals) to a new stack system; i.e. the new processes get their own global, local, and trail stack on which to execute. When both processes have terminated, the system will switch back to the original stack system. Possible results will remain on the global stack of the alternative stack systems and will not be copied back. (This affects only structured data objects since all atomic results would have been recorded in the original parent stack system anyway). Of course, should one process terminate before the other, execution cannot proceed with the next sequential goal since this goal might not be data independent from the still running parallel process. Consider the following example:

$$t(Y,U) \leftarrow s1(X,Y), s2(U), s3(X).$$

If we assume that the variables Y and U are bound to ground terms, then the goals s1 and s2 can be executed in parallel. However, should s2 terminate before s1 we cannot start executing s3, since s1 and s3 are not data independent. Hence, after a sequence of parallel executable goals we need a join operation. The join operator guarantees that no further goal is invoked until all parallel processes have terminated. The fork operator is a binary operator. If there are more than two goals that could be executed in parallel, the fork operation must be nested accordingly. For example, if three goals, g1, g2, and g3, can be executed concurrently they would be processed as fork(g1, fork(g2,g3)). In order to avoid an explosion of parallel processes (for example, in recursively forking programs such as quicksort), the number of available stack systems is restricted. If all stack systems are being used by parallel processes no new process can be forked. Only after some other parallel process has terminated can another process be spawned. Rather than queuing a process when no resources are available the fork operator will continue to execute the involved goals sequentially. This eliminates the overhead of queuing and dequeuing processes and prevents the system from breaking up into too many small processes. For example, the quicksort program would recursively fork until the only processes left are the leaf nodes. However, with finite resources it would have been much more advantageous to fork only a few times at the top level to saturate the system and then to execute sequentially within each parallel process without further forks.

To see how this concept is implemented on the presented processor pipeline, refer to the specification of the 'fork' instructions and to the annotated example in appendix B (quicksort). The basic principle is to inject another process into the pipeline. This is the reason why each pipeline buffer consists of several blocks. The number of blocks per pipeline buffer determines the maximal number of possible parallel processes.

3.4 Summary

An architecture has been presented that allows for the pipelined execution of sequential Prolog programs. A restricted form of AND- parallelism is also supported. Synchronization of access to shared data structures is handled in a uniform manner by controlling access to the respective stack pointers.

The execution model will be shortly summarized. To activate an idle processor one only needs to write an entry address into the appropriate buffer field. Whenever a processor has thus been activated by its left neighbor, the following three basic actions take place:[16]

1. The activated processor passes the received entry address to its instruction fetch unit to initiate an instruction prefetch sequence and - while the code is being fetched - copies its parent's environment pointer, choice point pointer, as well as the current local stack pointer into the next block of its right pipeline buffer (i.e., it copies the respective entries from the left buffer to the right buffer).

2. After a processor has thus been invoked, the parent processor starts copying - one by one - the arguments of the current goal into the pipeline buffer. When all the goal's arguments have been dispatched to the right processor, the left processor will stop and turn to the next block of its left pipeline buffer to see whether there are more goals to be processed.

3. If the called procedure provides several possible alternatives to solve the current goal, a choice point will be created on the local stack, and the last choice point pointer that has already been passed to the right processor will be updated. Also, the clause attempting to reduce the current goal might need to allocate an environment for its local variables. In this case a new environment is allocated on the local stack, and the new top of stack pointer is passed to the right pipeline buffer. Now it becomes clear why the last choice point pointer, the local stack pointer, and the environment pointer of the parent processor were passed to the right buffer as soon as the processor was invoked. At this point it was not known whether the current procedure would require a new choice point and/or environment. If no choice point and/or environment had been necessary, the old values of these pointers would have stayed valid. Note that the subsequent updating of the pointers after they have been passed to the right buffer is uncritical, since the right processor will not attempt to use them until an entry address

---

[16]the activating processor will be called the 'parent processor'

has been sent to the right processor. Only after the right neighbor has been activated is the left processor forbidden to modify already written buffer entries.

4 The Occur-Check Problem

4.1 Introduction

In Chapter 2 we have demonstrated how important unification with occur-check is. Unfortunately most Prolog implementations do not provide unification with occur-check due to the high overhead of carrying out the occur-check. The reason why this has not caused any more problems then it has is simple: in most cases the occur-check can safely be omitted since Prolog programs are ordinarily written in such a way as not to give rise to cyclic structures. Hence, the occur-check will only be necessary in those rare situations where cyclic structures might potentially result. If one could clearly indicate where the occur-check can safely be omitted and only execute the occur-check where necessary this would greatly reduce the overhead of 'sound' unification.

The question arises how to detect those places where the occur-check can be safely omitted and where an occur-check has to be made.[17] To find these places it helps to know that the occur-check is only necessary in those situations where a clause head literal *and* a clause body (goal) literal have more than one occurrence of any variable [Pl84]. Clause head literals are easily analysed since one only needs to check whether the respective variable names occur more than once within the head literal. However, variables within goal literals present a different situation. The problem is that these variables might have become aliased at an earlier time in the computation (i.e. they refer to the same storage location). It is therefore not sufficient just to look for goal literals in which a particular variable name occurs more than once. Consider the following example:

$$\ldots \, , \, g(X,Y), \, h(X,f(Y)), \, \ldots$$

$$g(Z,Z).$$
$$h(U,U).$$

In the above example unification with occur-check would fail because of an occur-check violation when variable U is unified with f(Y). Of course, to be on the safe side, one can always execute unification with occur-check whenever a variable occurs more than once in the clause head literal; thus meeting half the condition where an occur-check is necessary. Unfortunately whereas unbound variables rarely occur more than once within a *goal* literal this is not true for clause *head* literals. The 'doubling' of variables is a common (and sometimes necessary) technique for recursive Prolog procedures to pass the result back to the caller, as, for example, in the classical *append* procedure:

---

[17]One alternative, of course, is to have the user indicate the places where an occur-check should be executed: an unsatisfactory solution since it puts the burden on the user and is very error prone.

42

```
append([ ],X,X).
append([H|T],X,[H|T2]) :- append(T,X,T2).
```

If the decision whether an occur-check is necessary is based on the static structure of the clause head then the clause append([ ],X,X) requires unification with occur-check. Again, depending on how *append* is called this might require that an arbitrarily long list has to be traversed. However, *append* is rarely called in such a way that it might give rise to cyclic structures; hence *append* would not require unification with occur-check in most instances.

Sometimes there is additional static information available to further restrict the instances where unification with occur-check might be necessary. In his paper, Plaisted[Pl84] proposed a static global analysis of the Prolog program to detect those places where loops may be created and added appropriate checks at those places. However, like all static analyses the method is generally much too conservative and cannot consider Prolog's dynamic modification of procedures. For example, the clause append([ ],X,X) will again have to use unification with occur-check because a static analysis generally cannot rule out that the calling goal might be append([1],U,[1,U]) - a case which would result in an occur-check violation.

The core of the occur-check problem is the dynamic aliasing of variables. The hard part is to recognize at run-time whether a variable has been aliased or not. This aliasing problem is also at the heart of many synchronization problems (see Chapter 3). If a variable has not been aliased it can be bound without regard to other processes executing concurrently. By definition, a non-aliased variable provides only *one* access path to the variable's storage location, thus it cannot be manipulated by processes not in possession of this access path. Whenever this access path is duplicated or shared the variable becomes an aliased variable. Hence it is crucial to dynamically differentiate between aliased and non-aliased variables, both with regard to the occur-check problem and to avoid binding conflicts.

In the remainder of this chapter a method is presented for executing Prolog programs which avoids almost all unnecessary occur-checks. The method is based on a dynamic classification of the context in which logical variables occur, i.e. whether they are aliased or not. No static global analysis of the Prolog program is required to detect the places where an occur-check has to be made. The presented method has also an important side benefit: it greatly reduces the synchronization requirements to avoid binding conflicts in the parallel Prolog machine. Furthermore, it considerably cuts down on the number of memory references during the execution of Prolog programs - a very important aspect in a multi-processor environment with shared data memory. And, finally, in most cases it also avoids 'trailing' and 'untrailing' of unbound variables.

The proposed method will be discussed in terms of an actual implementation based on the Warren Abstract Prolog Instruction Set. However, the method should be applicable to other implementation models as well. It requires only the analysis of variable occurrences within a given clause - something every compiler has to do anyway. No assumptions are made with respect to a particular hardware or the Prolog architecture presented in the other parts of this thesis.

4.2   A Variable Classification Scheme

Prolog implementations - be they compiler or interpreter based systems - use data tags or descriptors to identify the objects to be unified. Those data types are 'atom', 'integer', 'structure' etc.; however, unbound logical variables are generally only tagged as 'unbound variable'. No further information is provided as to the context in which the variable occurs. This is where the presented scheme differs from other implementations. Through the use of further tags to identify aliased and non-aliased unbound variables and the context in which they occur, it is possible to avoid unecessary occur-checks. Only one extra data-tag will do the trick. However, this data tag will be interpreted differently by different instructions, thereby establishing a comprehensive way to express the context in which variables might occur.

Through a set of examples we will now develop a modified instruction set. The reader anxious to see the relevance for dealing with the occur-check problem should patiently bear with me. The solution to the occur-check problem will present itself in an almost trivial way at the end of the following discussion.

Let us first look at the traditional way variables are passed as arguments. Whenever an unbound variable occurs as a goal argument an unbound variable is created on either the local or global stack and the argument register is loaded with a reference to this location. The process of passing an unbound variable as a goal argument and the subsequent binding of the variable to a non-variable term can best be understood by looking at an example. Consider the following fragment of a Prolog program:

$$\ldots, g(X), \ldots$$

$$g(a) \leftarrow \ldots$$
$$g(b) \leftarrow \ldots$$

Assume the current goal is $g(X)$ and $g(X)$ is also the first goal in which the variable X occurs (i.e. the variable X is an unbound variable in the current goal). In order to resolve the current goal the following action takes place:

1. Create an unbound variable, X, in the current environment, place a pointer referencing variable X into the argument register, and call the procedure g.

2. Create a choice point for procedure g and unify the current goal with the unit clause $g(a)$. The unification process involves dereferencing the argument

register - yielding the unbound variable X- and binding variable X to 'a'. In this particular case the unbound variable X needs also to be trailed on the trail stack.

It seems to be a wasted effort to first create an unbound variable before invoking the current goal and then bind the variable immediately after the goal has been invoked. I propose to optimize the passing of unbound variables in the following way: instead of just having one 'tag' indicating whether a variable is unbound I introduce another 'tag' indicating that the variable is unbound but does not exist as a properly tagged unbound variable on either the local or global stack. This 'tag' is called 'NEW_UNBOUND'. I also distinguish between unbound variables on the local and global stack through appropriate 'tags', but this is only a minor optimization which is independent of the main scheme presented here. Execution of the above example would then proceed as follows:

1. Load a pointer to the location where the variable X is to reside into the argument register, 'tag' the argument register as 'NEW_UNBOUND'. *Do not* create an unbound variable at the location pointed to by the argument register. The location of variable X will stay undefined as of yet. Call procedure g.

2. Create a choice point for procedure g and unify the current goal with clause g(a). To bind the variable, just write the constant 'a' and the appropriate tag into the cell pointed to by the argument register.

In comparison with the first execution model the following steps have been saved:

- creation of an unbound variable,

- dereferencing of the argument register,

- the trail check,

- the trailing of the variable.

The question might arise why the trailing can be saved too. The reason is simple: the argument register contains the tag 'NEW_UNBOUND' and a pointer to an undefined cell. There is no need to trail an undefined memory cell; the fact that this cell represents an unbound variable is contained solely in the argument register which will be saved as part of the choice point anyway. In those cases where the variable would not have to be trailed we at least save checking whether it needs to be trailed. This scheme can be generalized even further. We do not explicitly establish variable-variable bindings any longer. Consider the following program:

$$?\text{-}\ g(X),\ \ldots$$

$$g(Y) \leftarrow t(U),\ s(Y).$$
$$s(a).$$

In the old model variable Y contains an explicit pointer (tagged as a reference) which points to the unbound variable X. In the new model the argument register of the current goal will just be saved in location Y and be restored when variable Y is used for the first time in the current clause body. When the variable Y is used for the first time in the clause body it still contains the tag 'NEW_UNBOUND' and a pointer to the variable X. Subsequent binding of Y will thus immediately cause the variable X to be bound without any dereferencing and trailing.

Of course there is a price to be paid. For the proposed scheme to work in all situations it is now necessary to explicitly handle void variables. Void variables are variables that occur only once within a given clause and can be considered dummy variables that will not be used further. In most Prolog implementations void variables that occur in the clause head will be ignored. Void variables that occur in the clause body cannot be ignored. Consider the following program:

$$?\text{-}g(X),t(X).$$

$$g(\_) \leftarrow \ldots$$
$$t(a) \leftarrow \ldots$$

When g(X) is invoked the variable X does not exist yet. (Remember only a pointer to the location of variable X is being passed as argument without really creating the variable X on the stack). However, when the goal t(X) is invoked we need to know the value of X. This causes no problem as long as the variable X will eventually become bound within the subtree spanned by the current goal g(X), because the binding will be written into the location of variable X. In the present case, however, variable X will not become bound within the subtree spanned by g(X). In order to give the variable X a value that can be used by the goal t(X) we need to put the cell representing the variable X into a well defined state. This is accomplished through a special instruction, 'get_void Ai'. The instruction 'get_void' examines the tag of the argument register Ai. If the tag is 'NEW_UNBOUND' an unbound variable will be created in the cell pointed to by the value field of the argument register. Otherwise 'get_void' behaves just like a NOOP instruction. In other words, the creation of unbound variables is delayed as long as possible in the hope that the variable will become bound before execution returns from the present computational subtree. It is only possible for an unbound variable to stay unbound within a computational subtree when the variable is unified with a void variable. In this case we do have to create an unbound variable on the stack in order to guarantee a well defined computational status upon return from the subtree. Of course, if a mode declaration indicates that the void variable would be matched with an instantiated input argument no instructions need to be generated for the void variable.

So far everything seems to be straightforward. However, to cover all possible situations one needs to look carefully at the context in which the variable occurs. Depending on the context the variable's tag needs to be changed or re-interpreted. Those situations are best explained through examples. The following examples will also provide a first glimpse into how Prolog clauses are actually compiled. So as not to confuse matters unnecessarily a sequential execution model will be used to explain the variable classification scheme and its implementation (the method applies just the same for the parallel execution model).

Example 1: Consider the following program fragment:

$$?- g(X), \ldots$$

$$g(Y) \leftarrow t(a), s(Y), h(Y).$$

which will translate into:

```
        put_var      X,A1
        call         g
        ⋮
g:      allocate     n
        move         A1,Y
        put_const    'a',A1
        call         t
        move         Y,A1
        call         s
        put_val      Y,A1
        deallocate
        execute      h
```

The current goal, g(X), contains an unbound variable. Hence, according to our new scheme, a pointer to the variable's location is loaded into the argument register. The pointer is tagged 'NEW_UNBOUND'. This is accomplished by the 'put_var' instruction. Note how the variable Y is treated in this example. In the clause head the argument register is saved in location Y. The variable Y now contains a pointer to the variable X (which does not exist yet) and the tag 'NEW_UNBOUND'. When the goal s(Y,U) is invoked the content of location Y is just copied into the argument register A1. However, when h(Y) is invoked the

47

content of location Y is still unchanged ('NEW_UNBOUND' and pointer to X). If this value is used as the argument of h(Y), the variable X might become bound again, disregarding any bindings established by the goal s(Y,U). However, in order to solve this problem the tag 'NEW_UNBOUND' need only be changed to 'REF'. A special instruction, 'put_value', just changes all 'NEW_UNBOUND' or 'UNBOUND' tags to 'REF'. In the above case the argument of h(Y) will now be a reference to location X. Since variable Y was used before in goal s(Y,U) it is guaranteed that the location of variable X will contain a proper value. (Remember that upon exit from a subtree all variables used in this subtree are in a well defined state). When procedure 'h' is called it will now have to dereference its argument to find out what the present value of variable X is.

Example 2:   Consider the following program fragment:

$$g \;\leftarrow\; t(X,X), \ldots$$

$$t(a,b) \;\leftarrow\; \ldots$$

which will translate into:

	put_local_ref	X,A1
	put_val	A1,A2
	call	t
t:	get_const	a,A1
	get_const	b,A2

If both argument registers of the goal t(X,X) were tagged 'NEW_UNBOUND', binding conflicts might arise later on. This is because 'NEW_UNBOUND' variables become bound directly without looking at the variable's location. When a variable occurs more than once within the calling goal it is always necessary to examine the variable's location before a particular binding is established, the reason being that in this case the same variable might be accessed (and hence bound) from different locations. Hence, if a variable, on its first occurrence in the clause body, occurs more than once in a goal we proceed as in the old model. An unbound variable is created and a reference to this variable is loaded into the argument register, thereby requiring the callee to always 'dereference' to the variable's location before attempting to bind the variable. This is accomplished through the instruction 'put_local_ref' which puts a reference to a local unbound variable into the argument register. (This instruction behaves exactly as the 'put_var' instruction of the old model).

Example 3:   Consider the following program fragment:

$$g(X) \leftarrow s(X,X), \ldots$$

which will translate into:

```
put_nonlocal_ref   A1,A1
put_val            A1,A2
call               s
```

As in the previous example, we cannot pass a dangling reference to the called procedure. However, we don't know the status of argument A1. It might be that the incoming argument A1 is a 'NEW_UNBOUND' variable which cannot be passed on as it is, due to the doubling of the variable X. The instruction 'put_nonlocal_ref' examines the tag of argument A1. If the argument type is 'NEW_UNBOUND' it will create the respective variable (similar to the 'get_void' instruction) and change the tag to 'REF' to reference the newly created variable. The difference between 'put_local_ref' and 'put_nonlocal_ref' is that the first always creates an unbound variable in the local environment while the latter examines the type of an argument that has come in through the clause head and only creates an unbound variable if the type of the head argument was 'NEW_UNBOUND'. But this 'NEW_UNBOUND' variable must lie in some earlier environment; hence the name 'put_nonlocal_ref'.

It should be mentioned that the 'doubling' of variables within a single goal is a very rare occurrence. According to our analysis of large Prolog programs this happens in less than 0.5% of all goals [Nö85].

4.3   Variables as Structure Arguments

The scheme of delaying the actual creation of unbound variables as long as possible can also be carried over to variables that occur within structures and/or lists (i.e. variables that would be created on the global rather than the local stack). Consider the following program fragment:

$$?- \ldots, g(X), \ldots$$

$$g(f(Y)) \leftarrow t(Y).$$

Assume the variable X is a new unbound variable. In this case the structure f(Y) needs to be created on the global stack. However, it is not necessary to also create an unbound variable Y on the global stack. It is sufficient to reserve a cell within the structure without actually initializing this cell to 'UNBOUND'. The reason is that if the structure f(Y) is unified with an argument register with tag type 'NEW_UNBOUND' we are guaranteed that this variable occurs only once within the calling goal. (Otherwise the tag would have been 'REF' with subsequent dereferencing yielding 'UNBOUND'). However, this implies that there exists only one pointer to the newly created structure f(Y) which lies outside of the present computational subtree. Hence, the structure can be left in a partially undefined state. It only needs to be guaranteed that the structure is in a well defined state when execution returns to the parent clause. For the above example this means that within the structure f(Y) the variable Y remains in an undefined state when the structure is created. When t(Y) is invoked, the argument register is loaded with a pointer to the undefined cell within the structure f( ) and the tag 'NEW_UNBOUND'. Now we can proceed as described in the other examples above. Whenever we return from the subtree spanned by t(Y), the undefined slot within the structure f() will have been put in a well defined state.

This whole scheme is implemented by providing another 'mode' flag. The Warren model provides two modes in which to execute certain instructions. If a structure within a clause head is being bound to a variable, the structure needs to be created. However, if the structure is matched with an already existing structure no new structure is created. There is only one set of instructions (established when the clause is compiled) that represent the structure. These 'structure instructions' can be executed in two modes - 'READ' mode (create the structure) and 'WRITE' mode (match the structure with an existing one). In the proposed new model the 'structure instructions' can also be executed in a 'WRITE_SAFE' mode. The 'WRITE_SAFE' mode indicates that the primary functor has been matched with an argument carrying a 'NEW_UNBOUND' tag, in which case the creation of variables within the structure can be safely delayed (i.e. the structure can remain partially undefined until we return to the parent clause). Of course, when a structure is created as a goal argument it must be completely defined. It is not permitted to have partially undefined structures as input arguments to procedures. To avoid dangling references within structures a new instruction was introduced. Consider the following Prolog clause:

$$g(f(x)) \leftarrow h(t(x)).$$
$$\Downarrow$$

get_structure	f,A1
unify_var	X
put_structure	t,A1
unify_unsafe_val	X
execute	h

Assume the structure f(X) is unified with an argument tagged 'NEW_UNBOUND'. Then the 'get_structure' instruction will set the mode to 'WRITE_SAFE' and the following 'unify_var' instruction will not create an unbound global variable, but only set the temporary variable X to 'NEW_UNBOUND' and a pointer to the undefined slot of the structure f(). However, when the structure t(X) is created, the value of the global variable X needs to be accessed. But this variable does not exist yet. Therefore a special instruction, 'unify_unsafe_val', is needed to bring the variable X into existence. It should be noted that in the following clause no special action is required:

$$g(f(x)) \leftarrow h(x).$$
$$\Downarrow$$

get_structure	f,A1
unify_var	A1
execute	h

The argument of the goal h(X) is just a pointer to the undefined slot of the structure f(X) with the tag 'NEW_UNBOUND'. As mentioned earlier, it is guaranteed that upon return from the goal h(X) everything involved in the computation of h(X) will be in a well defined state. In particular the empty slot of the structure f(X) must have been instantiated one way or the other.

One problem that has not been addressed yet is the 'aliasing' of variables (which, of course, is different from just passing a variable down a calling chain). However, this problem is trivial. Whenever two arguments with tag 'NEW_UN-BOUND' are unified, one variable will be created (i.e. tag 'UNBOUND' and value 'self reference'), and the other will be initialized to reference this variable and carry the tag 'REF'. Hence, we are back to the old Warren model.

The following table (Table 4-1) gives an indication of the savings in memory references by avoiding the explicit creation of unbound variables in memory, dereference, trail, and untrail operations. Actually the runtime savings are even greater, since in most cases checking whether a variable needs to be trailed can be dispensed with in our model. However, the runtime savings are very dependent on the machine architecture (e.g. how fast certain logical comparisons can be made and whether the involved object can be kept in registers). Therefore I have restricted myself to listing only the actual savings in memory references. The programs analysed are from a set of classical Prolog benchmark programs [Wa77/2] plus three other Prolog programs: 'append' (a list with 30 elements concatenated with a list with 1 element), '8-queens' and 'bucket'. (The programs are listed in Appendix A). The number of logical inferences (successful unifications) is also given. This number includes only unifications of user defined predicates. System predicates are compiled in-line. The reason for analysing this particular benchmark set and not large real world Prolog programs is that the savings of the new model depend on the programming style. The reader can judge for himself

program	unifications	operation	new model	old model
append	31	create unb variable	0	30
		deref	0	31
		trail	0	0
		untrail	0	0
naive rev.	496	create unb variable	0	465
		deref	0	466
		trail	0	0
		untrail	0	0
quicksort	376	create unb variable	50	478
		deref	50	479
		trail	0	225
		untrail	0	103
8-queens	2674	create unb variable	0	554
		deref	0	1001
		trail	0	673
		untrail	0	656
bucket	504	create unb variable	0	52
		deref	0	111
		trail	0	92
		untrail	0	58
palindrome	227	create unb variable	25	225
		deref	98	324
		trail	16	67
		untrail	0	35
query	127	create unb variable	0	127
		deref	644	1110
		trail	0	449
		untrail	0	440
times10	19	create unb variable	0	36
		deref	0	37
		trail	0	19
		untrail	0	0
divide10	19	create unb variable	0	54
		deref	0	55
		trail	0	19
		untrail	0	0
log10	11	create unb variable	0	10
		deref	0	11
		trail	0	11
		untrail	0	0
ops8	13	create unb variable	0	22
		deref	0	23
		trail	0	10
		untrail	0	0

Table 4-1: Comparison between the old and new model

to what extent the benchmark programs are representative of his/her application and/or programming style. The fact that substantial savings were obtained for all programs within the benchmark set should indicate the viability of the presented scheme. It should be pointed out that the new tag introduced to implement the presented scheme does not impose any run- time overhead as compared with the old Warren model (with the exception of the 'get_void' instruction which is not present in the old model). I have merely extended the set of possible tag values. However, the actions to be taken upon encountering a particular tag are determined by a switch table; branching to a particular action is independent of the table size (at least for small tables).

4.4   The Occur-Check Problem

By now it should be obvious how the presented variable classification scheme relates to the occur-check problem. Whenever a structure or list is matched against a variable with the tag 'NEW_UNBOUND' no occur-check needs to be executed since the tag 'NEW_UNBOUND' merely indicates that there can be no other pointer to the variable's storage location; hence, no loops can be created. However, whenever a structure or list is unified with a variable carrying the tag 'UNBOUND', the occur-check will have to be done. Aliasing of variables presents no problems. As we have seen in the discussion above whenever two 'NEW_UNBOUND' variables are unified with each other, both their tags will change. One variable will be set to 'UNBOUND' and the other to 'REF', referencing the other unbound variable.[18] Hence, aliased variables will always dereference to 'UNBOUND'. Therefore aliased variables require an occur-check when they are unified with structured data objects.

The actual places where the occur-check has to be included are straightforward. Consider the following cases:

i)   ← p(Z, s(Z)), ...

p(X, X).

ii)   ← p(Z, Z), ...

p(X, s(X)).

Since variable Z occurs more then once in the given goals it will carry the tag 'UNBOUND'. In example i) variable X will inherit the tag 'UNBOUND' of variable Z. When 'UNBOUND' variable X is subsequently unified with the structure

---

[18]It should be stressed again that this action does not represent an overhead compared with the old model.

s(Z) an occur-check will be executed. In example ii) the loop is created in the head of the called clause. The variable X will again inherit the tag 'UNBOUND' of variable Z. However, in this scenario - and this is particular to the Warren instruction set - when 'UNBOUND' variable Z is unified with the structure s(X) the occur-check is not executed right away. The variable Z will be set to point to the top of the global stack and execution will proceed in 'WRITE' mode, i.e. the structure s(X) will be created on the global stack by the code of the clause head (structure copying approach). Only when a variable which has previously been bound to a structure or list is encountered as part of the current structure will the occur-check be executed. This is the case in example ii). Variable X had been bound to Z, subsequently Z was bound to structure s(X). The structure was then copied onto the global stack. During the copying, variable X was encountered which (via Z) was bound to the structure s(Z); hence an occur-check had to be executed. This is a point where the presented scheme is too conservative and always assumes the worst case. Consider the following example:

$$\ldots, p(\ s(a),\ Y,\ Y\ ),\ \ldots$$

$$p(\ Z,\ U,\ s(\ Z\ )\ ) \leftarrow \ldots$$

Since variable Y occurs more than once in the current goal it would carry the tag 'UNBOUND'. Variable Z is bound to s(a); however, when copying s(Z) onto the global stack it is not known that the variable Z and its structure pointer to s(a) does not point back into the current structure s(Z), thereby creating a loop. In this situation an unnecessary occur-check would be executed. This situation can only be ruled out through a global data analysis of the program. It should be noted that if variable Y had occured only once within the given goal no occur-check would have resulted. In this case Y would have been a 'NEW_UNBOUND' variable and Y could have been safely bound to s(Z) without occur-check. The reader can easily convince himself that the presented scheme is also independent of the order in which the arguments are unified.

Table 4-2 shows a comparison between the old and the new model with occur-check included. None of the benchmark programs require an occur-check for their correct execution. As can be seen from Table 4-2, in all but one program does the new execution model detect automatically that no occur-check is necessary. It is interesting to investigate why in one case the new method failed to detect an unnecessary occur-check. Consider the program where the method failed:

```
quicksort([ ],X,X).
quicksort([H|T],R,R0)  ←   split(T,H,Sm.Lrg),
                           quicksort(Sm,R,[H|R1]),
                           quicksort(Lrg,R1,R0).
```

program	new model	old model
append	0	1
naive reverse	0	30
quicksort	49	50
8-queens	0	341
bucket	0	90
palindrom	0	95
query	0	0
times10	0	8
divide10	0	16
log10	0	9
ops8	0	4

Table 4-2: Number of times the occur-check routine has to be invoked

As mentioned above, structures that occur as goal arguments have to be completely defined before they are passed to the called procedure. Hence, the list [H|R1] cannot be left partially undefined. However, the variable R1 will never become instantiated within this recursive call. This fact is unknown to the call quicksort(Lrg,R1,R0) and, therefore, the variable R1 cannot be passed down as a 'NEW_UNBOUND' variable. The respective argument register must be loaded with a pointer to R1's location and a tag 'REF'. The called procedure must then dereference the respective argument, yielding an unbound variable, R1. Given the tag 'UNBOUND', rather then 'NEW_UNBOUND', the called procedure must make a worst case assumption about the context of the unbound variable. Hence, when the variable is subsequently bound to a structure an occur-check needs to be executed. If the same program had been written in the following form:

```
quicksort([ ],[ ]).
quicksort([H|T],R)  ←   split(T,H,Sm.Lrg),
                        quicksort(Sm,R1,),
                        quicksort(Lrg,R2),
                        append(R1,[H|R2],R).
```

no occur-check would have been executed.

The numbers given in Table 4-2 are the number of times the occur- check would have to be invoked and not the number of memory references made within one occur-check invocation. This was done in order to avoid any assumptions about the actual implementation of the occur- check routine itself since the occur-check algorithm very strongly depends on the internal data representation. For example, in some cases the occur-check in the Warren model becomes quite simple. When a variable dereferences to a location on the local stack this variable can be bound to a structure or list without further occur-checks. This is because of the stack organization of the Warren model. There can be no pointers from the global stack into the local stack. Hence, the structure/list being processed cannot contain the local variable. Even so, it is safe to say - by a comparison of Table 4-1 and Table 4-2 - that in terms of necessary memory references the new model with occur-check should execute faster then the old model without occur-check. The few unnecessary occur-checks that are still being executed even in the new model are more than compensated for by the savings in memory references in the new model.

4.5   Summary

In summary, the proposed scheme allows one to differentiate at runtime between variables that occur once and more than once in a given goal. This information helps to decide whether a variable is possibly aliased or not. Whenever un-aliased variables are unified with arbitrary terms the occur-check can safely be omitted and unification becomes a simple assignment operation.

Being able to distinguish between aliased and un-aliased variables has many important side benefits. In most cases un-aliased variables do not need to be explicitly created on the stack and they don't need to be 'trailed' upon binding. Furthermore, if a structure within a clause head is unified with an unbound variable which occurs only once within the calling goal the structure can safely be left partially undefined until control is passed back to the parent clause. All these savings in memory references contribute greatly to the performance of the parallel Prolog machine. Variables that can be guaranteed to be un-aliased also greatly reduce the synchronization requirements of concurrently executing unification operations.

5 The Abstract Parallel Prolog Machine

This chapter provides the complete specification of the abstract parallel Prolog instruction set and the processor architecture. The machine instructions of the parallel Prolog machine are based on the Warren abstract Prolog instruction set [Wa83]; however, the original instruction set proposed by D.H.D Warren has been changed and optimized to conform to the parallel execution model.

For those readers who are familiar with the Warren abstract Prolog instruction set I will briefly outline the major differences:

1. The new instruction set does not allow to dynamically trim the environment after every procedure call.[19] Dynamic environment trimming causes the same problems as tail recursion optimization (see Chapter 3); however, the impact on the pipeline flow is more severe since it might affect every call, rather than just the last call within a clause body. Therefore I have chosen not to support dynamic environment trimming.

2. The new instruction set distinguishes between global and local variables. This makes checking the trail condition easier and does not require the local and global stack to be in a particular order with respect to each other.

3. The new instruction set supports special tags to indicate whether variables might have been aliased (see Chapter 4).

4. The new instruction set has slightly different clause control and *switch* instructions. However, this is only a minor design decision.

5. Of course, all control flow instructions have been changed to conform to the pipeline execution model.

Despite all these changes I feel the instruction set has retained the spirit of the original Warren Prolog instruction set. However, as mentioned before, there are many alternative ways to compile Prolog programs. I have chosen to base the architecture on the Warren Prolog instruction set, because it was one of the first fully documented instruction sets, and the ideas put forward by Warren have had a tremendous influence on the construction of Prolog compilers.

5.1 Data Representation

The parallel Prolog machine is a tagged architecture. The data tags are used to identify the data objects to be worked on and to establish the context in

---

[19]Dynamic environment trimming is a generalization of tail recursion optimization. After every call those variables in the environment that will not be used anymore can be discarded, i.e. the environment can be compacted. The same restrictions as for tail recursion optimization apply.

which generic instructions are to be executed in a given instance. Rather than extending the machine word width to accomodate the data tag (as the Symbolics LISP machine does) I opted to use the most significant 5 bits of a standard 32 bit word to represent the tag field. It is important for a coprocessor architecture to stay within the standard word size of the host computer in order to avoid compatibility problems. Hence a tagged data object has the following layout:

$$< tag(bits31..27)|value(bits26..0) >$$

It should be noted that not all objects are tagged. Absolute code addresses, stack pointers, etc., are, of course, not tagged. Generally one can say that only the Prolog specific data objects are tagged. At this point the parallel Prolog machine knows the following data objects:

INTEGER: tag = INT, value = numerical value of the integer

ATOM: tag = ATOM, value = a pointer into the symbol table where the ASCII string of the atom is stored

NIL: value = none. A special object without value representing the empty list.

STRUCTURE POINTER: tag = STRUC, value = a pointer to a Prolog structure on the global stack (to be explained shortly).

LIST POINTER: tag = LIST,
value = a pointer to a list cell on the global stack

GLOBAL_UNBOUND: tag = GLOBAL_UNB, value = a pointer to itself. Standard representation of an unbound variable on the global stack.

LOCAL_UNBOUND: tag = LOCAL_UNB, value = a pointer to itself. Standard representation of an unbound variable on the local stack.

NEW_GLOBAL_UNBOUND: tag = NEW_GLOBAL, value = a pointer to an uninitialized cell on the global stack which represents a variable.

NEW_LOCAL_UNBOUND: tag = NEW_LOCAL, value = a pointer to an uninitialized cell on the local stack which represents a variable.

REFERENCE: tag = REF, value = a pointer to a variable cell. The cell pointed to must be in a well defined state.

The present number of different tags does not require a 5 bit tag field. However, the remaining bits of the 5 bit tag are reserved for future use (e.g. double precision arithmetic and floating point numbers, etc.). Having reserved the most significant 5 bits of a 32 bit word means of course that addresses are restricted to being at most 27 bits long. However, an address space of 128 Mbyte should be more than sufficient.

The representation of Prolog structures like f(a,t(b),X) where f is the functor, 'a' an atom, X a variable, and t(b) an embedded substructure is shown in Figure 5-1. It is important to note that structures and lists can only be accessed via structure or list pointers respectively. Hence it is sufficient to tag only the access pointers. However, the individual structure or list elements are tagged according to their type. The first word of a structure always contains the primary functor of the structure and its arity (i.e. the number of arguments of the structure). The functor is represented as a pointer to the symbol table containing the ASCII string of the functor. The arity is stored in the tag field. All the arguments of the structure are allocated in consecutive order.

Lists are constructed out of two element list cells. The first element is the list head and the second element is the list tail. The list head can be any Prolog data object; however, the list tail must be either the empty list or a another list pointer, i.e. a list [a,b,c] is represented as (a,(b(c,NIL))). This is also the standard list representation for many other programming languages. Figure 5-2 shows the representation of a list.

5.2 Registers and Status Flags

The processors of the parallel Prolog machine have the following internal registers:

my_gpos: an internal copy of the global stack pointer,

my_tpos: an internal copy of the trail stack pointer,

my_env: a pointer to the current environment,

my_chpnt: a pointer to the current choice point,

Nextarg: a pointer to the next argument of a structured data object,

temp1,2: auxiliary registers.

The pipeline registers of a pipeline buffer block are:

Entry: The entry address of the next goal or procedure.

Size: The size of the current buffer block (number of goal arguments plus control words).

Lpos: The current local stack pointer.

Tpos: The current trail stack pointer.

Gpos: The current stack pointer of the global stack.

Nextclause: A pointer to the next clause to consider upon backtracking.

GLOBAL STACK

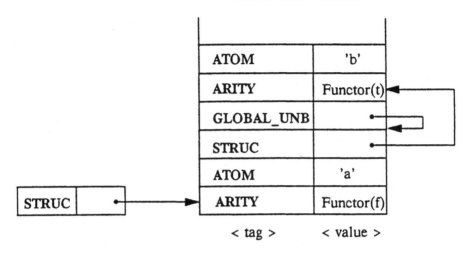

Figure 5-1: Representation of the structure f(a,t(b),X)

GLOBAL STACK

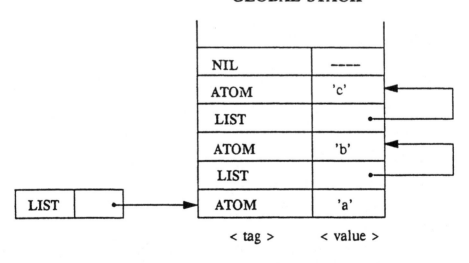

Figure 5-2: Representation of the list (a,(b,(c,NIL)))

60

Currenv: A pointer to the current environment.

Continst: The current return address.

A1..Ai: The current argument registers.

Additionally each pipeline buffer block also contains four communication status flags:

DONE will be set when the left neighbor has completed writing into the current pipeline buffer block.

PROCEED indicates whether the left neighbor is still accessing an already discarded environment. Necessary to implement tail recursion optimization.

RLTPOS indicates whether the left neighbor has released the trail stack pointer.

RLGPOS indicates whether the left neighbor has released the stack pointer to the global stack pointer.

To distinguish between left and right pipeline buffer the registers and status bits will be prefixed 'L_' or 'R_' respectively. Argument registers are not always prefixed since a processor can use both the left and the right argument registers. The processor itself contains the following implementation specific status bits:

COPY_CHPNT indicates whether a choice point needs to be copied to or from the local stack.

BACKTRACK_STATUS indicates whether deep or shallow backtracking is to take place upon a Prolog 'fail' operation.

IN_POSSESSION_OF_TPOS indicates whether the processor has already possession of the trail stack pointer.

IN_POSSESSION_OF_GPOS indicates whether the processor has already possession of the stack pointer of the global stack.

RELEASE_TPOS indicates that the processor does not need the trail stack pointer any longer.

RELEASE_GPOS indicates that the processor does not need the pointer to the global stack any longer.

MODE establishes the context in which certain instructions have to be executed (i.e. create a new structure, match an already existing one, or be able to leave a structure in an undefined state).

5.3 The Parallel Instruction Set

The instructions of the proposed parallel Prolog machine can be grouped into 6 main groups according to their functionality:

Control Instructions The instructions in this group comprise the Prolog specific low level memory management and control flow instructions. The instructions are: *Allocate, Deallocate, Proceed, Execute*, and *Call*.

Goal Instructions The instructions in this group serve to set the argument register prior to a subgoal invocation.

Clause Head Instructions The instructions in this group unify the formal arguments of the clause head with the actual parameters of the calling goal. The instructions that represent structured data objects occurring in the clause head can be executed in one of three modes (*read, write*, or *wite_safe* mode) depending on the type of the actual argument with wgich they are matched.

Structure Instructions The instructions in this group process the components of structured data objects. A sequence of structure instructions must always be preceded by an instruction (either a clause head or a goal instruction) which establishes the type of the structure to be worked on as well as the execution mode (*read/write/write_safe* mode). If the structure has to be created (*write* mode), this instruction will also reserve space for the structure on the global stack. Embedded substructures are compiled in exactly the same manner as in the old Warren model, with one exception: structures occurring in the clause head which will always have to be created, can be created through a set of special instructions that allocate sufficient space on the global stack and then create the structure components in an *arbitrary* order. (That a structure occurring in the clause head must always be created can, of course, be known only through mode declarations). This is a subtle and highly specialized optimization for the parallel Prolog machine. However, these instructions will not be explained further since they do not provide any new insight and can easily be derived from the current set of instructions.[20]

Clause Control Instructions The instructions in this group control the access to the clauses of a procedure. They establish the selection order in which the alternative clauses should be selected for execution, and control the Prolog backtrack mechanism. The clause control instructions can be split into two groups:

1. The purpose of *Choice Point Management Instructions* is to implement the backtrack mechanism. Whenever a non-deterministic procedure is entered,

---

[20]See Appendix B for an example on how these instructions are used.

a choice point will be established by a single instruction, *try*. Another instruction, *retry*, is responsible for updating the choice point every time backtracking to an alternative clause takes place; however, when the last alternative is being considered, then the pool of clauses for this procedure has been exhausted, and the procedure's choice point must be discarded. The *trust* instruction releases the choice point prior to entering the last alternative clause.

2. The purpose of *Filter Instructions* is to filter out those clauses of a given procedure that can not possibly unify with the current goal. The main instructions of this group are:

switch_on_term	Lv, Lc, Ll, Ls
switch_on_constant	N, Table
switch_on_structure	N, Table

This filtering is done dynamically at run-time and is based on a type compatability check between the first parameter of the calling goal and the first arguments of the clauses belonging to the called procedure. Consider the following subgoal invocation:

?-g(X).

g([a,b]) :- ...
g([c,d]) :- ...
g(a) :- ...
g(b) :- ...

The clause control instructions for procedure g(...) would look as follows:

```
         switch_on_term        Lv, Lc, Ll, Ls

Lv:  try                 C1
     retry               C2
     retry               C3
     trust               C4


Lc:  switch_on_constant  2, (C3, C4)

Ll:  try                 C1
     trust               C2


Ls:  fail
```

The *switch_on_term* instruction examines the type of the first parameter of the calling goal (in this case X). If X is an unbound variable, all clauses of procedure *g* can match the calling goal, since an unbound variable cannot cause the unification to fail. If X is a constant (or is bound to a constant), *switch_on_term* will branch to label Lc, where the *switch_on_constant* will further examine the actual parameter X and select either clause C3 or C4 (or fail) for execution. If X is a list (or bound to a list), only the clauses C1 and C2 could possibly unify the calling goal. Finally, if X is a structure (or bound to a structure), an immediate fail will result without even trying to unify any of the clauses with the current goal.

AND-Parallel Instructions   These instructions are support instructions and facilitate the concurrent execution of goals that meet the criteria for AND-parallel execution.

Miscellaneous Instructions   These instructions are support instructions, to enable the in-line execution of built-in predicates such as the CUT. There are also instructions that are specific to the proposed pipeline machine (e.g. release stack pointer, copy data from right to the left pipeline buffer,etc.).

All instructions consist of a 1Byte op-code and zero, one, or two operands. The operands are either 1Byte or 4Bytes in size. Pipeline buffer block addresses are all 1Byte addresses. The left pipeline buffer block has the addresses 0..31 and the right pipeline buffer block has addresses 32..63. The addressing modes are very simple and are completely encoded in the op-code. Hence, if an instruction can be used in two different addressing modes we have in effect two different instructions. This greatly simplifies the decoding of the instructions. All instructions are byte alligned (see Chapter 6.2.3 'Instruction Fetch Unit' for further details). Instead of distinguishing between INTEGER and ATOM constants I introduced a new tag, CONST, to cover both cases to keep the specification short. (The operations invoked by an INTEGER or ATOM data object are - except for certain built-in predicates - symetric).

A few words about the pseudo code in which I described the operational semantics of each abstract instruction. The '<--' operator is the assignment operator: it accomplishes the transfer of data between registers or registers-memory transfers. The setting (and testing) of status flags is denoted through the '=' operator to distinguish this operation from data transfer operations. The MEM(...) function is an indirection operator. The function MEM(...) can be used either as the source or the destination of a data transfer. In the first case the argument of MEM will be interpreted as an address, and the value returned is the contents of the memory word addressed by the argument. If the function MEM is the destination of a data transfer, the argument is interpreted as the address of the memory word that is to receive the data object. In both cases the argument can be either a register or a memory word whose content will be interpreted as an address.

Tagged data objects will be represented in the following way: $< tag|value >$. The construct TAG.object or VALUE.object accesses the tag field or the value field, respectively, of a tagged object. If an instruction can be used in two different addressing modes I used a generic operand, 'Vn'. This was done in order to avoid having to provide the specification of two instructions that differ only in their addressing mode. Depending on the addressing mode this operand can either be an offset into the current environment or the address of an argument register. In both cases Vn will be a 1Byte operand. If Vn is an offset into the current environment all operations involving Vn have to be replaced by MEM(my_env+Vn). Otherwise Vn represents an argument register and can be used directly.

All pipeline registers and status bits are prefixed L_ or R_ indicating the left or right pipeline buffer respectively. Instruction operands that address argument registers are denoted as Ai. The actual value of the operand determines whether the left or right buffer was meant.

There are three micro-routines that will be used by many of the other instructions and must therefore be briefly explained.

GET_TPOS: This routine is invoked when an instruction needs the trail stack pointer from the left pipeline buffer. If the processor already has possession of the trail stack pointer, the routine is ignored. Otherwise, the micro-routine tries to obtain the trail stack pointer (it will automatically delay if the pointer has not yet been written into the pipeline buffer block). When the stack pointer becomes available it is copied into a local processor register and a flag is set to indicate that the processor now has possession of the trail stack pointer.

```
1   IF  IN_POSESSION_OF_TPOS='NO'  THEN
2       my_tpos  <--  L_Tpos
3       IN_POSESSION_OF_TPOS = 'YES'
4       L_RLTPOS            = 'NO'
5   ENDIF
```

GET_GPOS: This routine is basically identical to the micro routine above. However, the stack pointer in question is the pointer to the top of the global stack

```
1   IF  IN_POSESSION_OF_GPOS='NO'  THEN
2       my_gpos  <--  L_Gpos
3       IN_POSESSION_OF_GPOS = 'YES'
4       L_RLGPOS            = 'NO'
5   ENDIF
```

WAIT_UNTIL_SAFE(Label,X): This routine has to be invoked when an instruction tries to bind an unbound variable, X. To avoid binding conflicts the processor has to obtain the trail stack pointer before the binding can be established. If the processor has already possession of the trail pointer the 'WAIT_UNTIL_SAFE' routine is bypassed. Otherwise this routine tries to obtain the trail pointer. However, by the time it has obtained the trail pointer it cannot be guaranteed anymore that the variable in question is still unbound. Hence, we must look at the variable's location to determine its present status. (The register X still contains the address of the variable in its value field. Remember, unbound variables contain a self-reference in their value field). After having loaded register X again, the instruction that invoked the 'WAIT...' routine is re-executed. (Label is a micro-program label referencing the beginning of the micro-sequence of the current instruction).

```
1   IF IN_POSSESSION_OF_TPOS = 'NO' THEN
2       my_tpos  <--  L_Tpos
3       L_RLTPOS = 'NO'
4       IN_POSSESSION_OF_TPOS = 'YES'
5       X  <--  MEM( VALUE.X )
6       goto Label
7   ENDIF
```

5.3.1   Control Instructions

allocate   n

This instruction appears at the beginning of a clause with more than one goal in the body. The parameter 'n' determines the size of the environment to be allocated on the local stack. If the 'PROCEED' status of the left pipeline buffer block is set, execution delays until the 'PROCEED' status is reset. The current top of the local stack (contained in pipeline register L_Lpos) becomes the base pointer of the new environment. The pipeline registers, L_Continst and L_Currenv, are saved as part of the new environment. The new environment pointer and the new top of stack (environment base + size) are passed to the right processor.

```
1   Wait until L_PROCEED = 'YES'
2   my_env                <--   L_Lpos
3   MEM(my_env)           <--   L_Currenv
4   MEM(my_env+1)         <--   L_Continst
5   R_Currenv             <--   my_env
6   R_Lpos                <--   my_env + n
```

deallocate

This instruction appears before the final execute instruction in a clause with more than one goal in the body (i.e. a clause for which an environment had to be allocated). The return address is restored and temporarily saved in the respective left pipeline register. The subsequent *execute* instruction will pass the return address to the right neighbor. The pointer to the previous environment is also restored and passed to the right neighbor (i.e the current environment has been logically discarded). However, if there are choice points that lie above the environment to be discarded the occupied memory space cannot be released. Backtracking might cause the environment to be re-activated. Otherwise the memory space is released (i.e. the environment base pointer becomes the new top of stack) and the updated stack pointer is passed to the right neighbor. However, due to the tail recursion optimization, the processor executing the *deallocate* instruction might still access the discarded environment. Therefore the right neighbor needs to be temporarily disabled from immediately overwriting the released stack space. This is accomplished by setting the *PROCEED* status of the right pipeline buffer to 'NO'.

```
1   R_Currenv     <--   MEM(my_env)
2   L_Continst    <--   MEM(my_env+1)
3   IF  my_chpnt < my\_env   THEN
4       R_Lpos      <--   my_env
5       R_PROCEED   =   'NO'
6   ENDIF
```

call   Label1, Label2

This instruction issues a call to solve the current body goal. If the clause body goal consists of only one goal or the current goal is the last goal of the body, the *execute* instruction should be used. The entry address of the called procedure and the return address are passed to the right neighbor processor.

```
1   R_Entry      <--   Label1
2   R_Continst   <--   Label2
```

execute   Label

The instruction issues a call to solve the final (or only) goal of a clause body. The entry address of the called procedure and the value of the *PROCEED* status bit are passed to the right neighbor. Since there are no other goals to be solved within the current clause no explicit return address for the current clause is provided. The return address is determined dynamically from the current value of the return address register, *Continst*. The current value of this register is passed to the right neighbor. Note that a preceding *deallocate* instruction might have restored the register L_Continst to provide the entry address of the next goal. This goal, of course, belongs to a clause body one level up in the search tree.

```
1   R_PROCEED    =    L_PROCEED
2   R_Entry      <--  Label
3   R_Continst   <--  L_Continst
```

proceed

This instruction causes the return from a unit clause. It passes the current return address to the right neighbor processor where it will serve as the start address of the next goal to be processed.

```
1   R_PROCEED    =    L_PROCEED
2   R_Entry      <--  L_Continst
```

stop

This instruction terminates execution of the current code block. The processor waits until its left neighbor has terminated and resets all status bits. Note that the *PROCEED* flag is now set to 'YES' indicating that all processors to the right can now allocate new environments and/or choice points. Of course, this is only relevant if a previous *deallocate* instruction has set the flag to 'NO'. The default setting of this flag is 'YES' anyway. After having reset all status registers the processor waits for a new entry address where to start execution (line 14). When a new entry address has been obtained, the registers L_Currenv, L_Last_chpnt, and L_Lpos are immediately passed to the right neighbor. Remember that those registers are guaranteed to be present. They must have been set by the left neighbor prior to setting the L_Entry.

```
1    Wait until (L_DONE = 'YES')
2    L_DONE      = 'NO'
3    L_RLTPOS    = 'NO'
4    L_RLGPOS    = 'NO'
5    R_PROCEED   = 'YES'
6    R_DONE      = 'YES'
7    reset_left_buffer
8    increment_block_counter
9    BACKTRACK_STATUS        = 'DEEP'
10   IN_POSSESSION_OF_GPOS   = 'NO'
11   IN_POSSESSION_OF_GPOS   = 'NO'
12   RELEASE_GPOS            = 'NO'
13   COPY_CHPNT              = 'NO'
14   PC                      <--  R_Entry
15   R_Currenv, my_env       <--  L_Currenv
16   R_Last_chpnt, my_chpnt  <--  L_Last_chpnt
17   R_Lpos                  <--  L_Lpos
```

complete_chpnt

This instruction copies a choice point from the current pipeline buffer block onto the local stack. Space to accomodate the choice point was reserved by a previous *try* instruction. Due to the dynamic behavior of Prolog it cannot always be determined whether it is really necessary to save the choice point. The status bit COPY_CHPNT indicates whether the choice point has to be saved.

```
1    Wait until L_PROCEED = 'YES'
2    IF  COPY_CHPNT = 'YES'  THEN
3       temp  <--  2
4       FOR  i=0  TO  n  DO
5          MEM(my_chpnt+i)  <--  L_Buffer(temp)
```

```
6          temp  <--  temp + 1
7      ENDFOR
8  ENDIF
```

5.3.2 Goal Instructions

put_var   n,Ai

This instruction represents the first occurrence of a variable, X, as a goal argument.
The location of the variable is given as an offset, n, from the current environment.
The variable X does not occur in the clause head and the variable occurs only once
within the current goal. If the variable occurs more than once within the respective
goal, the "put_local_ref" instruction must be used. The argument register Ai is
initialized with a tag 'NEW_UNBOUND' and a pointer to the variable's location
in memory. The variable's location in memory remains undefined.

```
1   Ai  <--  <NEW_LOCAL|my_env+n>
```

put_global_var   Ai

This instruction is a special case of the instruction above. The instruction represents an unbound variable that occurs as a goal argument of the last goal of
the clause body and it occurs in the last goal only once; therefore it could also be
interpreted as a goal 'void variable'. If the variable occurs more than once as an argument of the last goal the *put_global_ref* instruction must be used. GET_GPOS
is a micro-program routine to obtain the stack pointer of the global stack (see
5.3). Register Ai is loaded with a tag, 'NEW_GLOBAL' and the stack pointer of
the global stack. The global stack pointer is incremented.

```
1   GET_GPOS
2   Ai       <--   <NEW_GLOBAL|my_gpos>
3   my_gpos  <--   my_gpos+1
```

put_local_ref   n,Ai

For this instruction to be used, the following conditions must hold: the instruction
must represent the first occurrence of a variable, X, as a goal argument, the
variable must occur more than once within the respective goal, and the variable
must not have occured in the clause head. In this case an unbound variable is
created on the local stack and the argument register is initialized to reference the
unbound variable.

```
1   MEM(my_env+n)  <--   <LOCAL_UNB|my_env+n>
2   Ai             <--   <REF|my_env+n>
```

70

put_nonlocal_ref   Vn,Ai

For this instruction to be used, the following conditions must hold: the instruction must represent the first occurrence of a variable, Vn, as a goal argument, the respective goal must contain the variable more than once, and the variable must have occurred once within the clause head. If register Ai is a pointer with tag 'NEW_UNBOUND', the variable pointed to will be brought into existence, and variable 'Vn' will be set to reference this newly created variable. This instruction has two addressing modes: the operand Vn is either an offset into the current environment - addressing an environment variable - or an argument register address. In both cases is the operand one byte long. If Vn represents an environment variable, then (Vn) stands for MEM(my_env+Vn) to access the variable's location. Otherwise (Vn) is the content of the respective argument register.

```
 0   GET_TPOS      /* Only necessary if Vn is an environment
                                  variable */
 1   temp  <--  (Vn)
 2   CASE  TAG.temp  OF
 3      NEW_LOCAL   : MEM(temp) <--  <LOCAL_UNB|temp>
 4                    Ai        <--  <REF|temp>
 5      NEW_GLOBAL  : MEM(temp) <--  <GLOBAL_UNB|temp>
 6                    Ai <--  <REF|temp>
 7      LOCAL_UNB,
 8      GLOBAL_UNB  : Ai <--  <REF|temp>
 9      OTHERWISE   : Ai <--  temp
10   ENDCASE
```

put_global_ref   Ai

This instruction represents an unbound variable that occurs more than once as a goal argument of the last goal of a clause. The stack pointer to the global stack is obtained and an unbound variable is created on the global stack. A pointer to this variable is loaded into register Ai. For the other argument positions of this variable the argument register Ai will then be copied into the respective argument registers through a *put_value* (or *move reg, reg*) instruction.

```
 1   GET_GPOS
 2   MEM(my_gpos)     <--  <GLOBAL_UNB|my_gpos>
 3   Ai               <--  <REF|my_gpos>
 4   my_gpos          <--  my_gpos+1
```

put_value   Vn,Ai

This instruction represents a goal argument that is a bound variable. The variable, Vn, has occurred either previously within the clause body, or has occurred more than once within the clause head. If the value of the variable is still 'UNBOUND' or 'NEW_UNBOUND', the instruction will change the tag to 'REF' and load register Ai with the value of variable Vn. If the variable has occurred only once in the clause head, its first occurrence within the clause body will be handled through either a *move* instruction (if the variable occurs only once within the goal) or a *put_nonlocal_ref* instruction. Only subsequent occurrences of the variable in later goals will be processed by the *put_value* instruction.

```
0   GET_TPOS       /* Only necessary if Vn is an environment
                                  variable */
1   Ai  <--  (Vn)
2   CASE  TAG.Ai  OF
3      NEW_LOCAL,
4      NEW_GLOBAL,
5      GLOBAL_UNB,
6      LOCAL_UNB  :  TAG.Ai  <--   REF
7      OTHERWISE  :  Continue
6   ENDCASE
```

put_unsafe_value   n,Ai

This instruction represents a variable in the last goal of the clause body with the additional condition that the variable did not occur in the clause head or as an argument of a structure. Variables for which these conditions hold are called *unsafe* variables. If one of these conditions does not apply, a simple *put_value* instruction can be used. The reason for the special treatment of unsafe variables lies in the implementation of the tail recursion optimization. If the variable dereferences to an uninstantiated variable within the current environment, this variable needs to be 'globalized'. No pointer to the variable (i.e. into the current environment) can be passed to the called procedure since the stack space of the environment might be released, thereby creating a dangling reference. Hence, the variable is put onto the global stack where it has a longer lifetime. The old location of the variable is set to point to the variable's new location on the global stack. This is necessary since the old location might still be accessed after backtracking.

```
1   temp  <--  MEM(my_env + n)
2   CASE  TAG.temp  OF
3      REF      :  temp  <--  MEM(VALUE.temp)
4                  Goto 2
5      LOCAL_UNB:  IF  VALUE.temp > my_env  THEN
6                      WAIT_UNTIL_SAFE(2,temp)
```

```
7                    TRAIL_LOCAL(temp)
8                    GET_GPOS
9                    MEM(my_gpos) <-- <GLOBAL_UNB|my_gpos>
10                   Ai              <-- <REF|my_gpos>
11                   MEM(VALUE.temp) <-- Ai
12                   my_gpos <-- my_gpos + 1
13              ELSE
14                   Ai <-- temp
15     OTHERWISE: Ai <-- temp
16   ENDCASE
```

put_const   'C', Ai

This instruction represents a goal argument that is a constant. The instruction
simply puts the constant C into register Ai.

```
Ai  <--  <CONST|'C'>
```

put_nil   Ai

This instruction represents a goal argument that is the special constant NIL. NIL
represents an empty list.

```
Ai  <--  <NIL|_>
```

put_structure   F, Ai

This instruction marks the beginning of a structure occurring as a goal argument.
The instruction pushes the functor F for the structure onto the global stack,
and puts a corresponding structure pointer into register Ai. The stack pointer
of the global stack is incremented to reserve sufficient space for the structure to
be created. The subsequent 'structure instructions' will build up the structure
starting at the location pointed to by register Nextarg. Execution proceeds in
'WRITE' mode.

```
1   GET_GPOS
2   MEM(my_gpos)    <-- F
3   Ai              <-- <STRUCTURE|my_gpos>
4   Nextarg         <-- my_gpos + 1
5   my_gpos         <-- Nextarg + Arity(F)
6   MODE            =  'WRITE'
```

put_last_structure   F, Ai

This instruction marks the beginning of the last structured object within a goal. Hence, the global stack pointer can be released after stack space for the structure has been reserved. The instruction is an optimized version of the *put_structure* instruction. The following changes have to be made to the specification of the *put_structure* instruction:

```
5    R_Gpos          <-- Nextarg + Arity(F)
6    MODE            = 'WRITE'
7    R_RLGPOS        = 'YES'
```

put_list   Ai

This instruction is a special case of the *put_structure* instruction. The structure in question is a list.

```
1    GET_GPOS
2    Ai              <-- <LIST|my_gpos>
3    Nextarg         <-- my_gpos
4    my_gpos         <-- my_gpos + 2
5    MODE            = 'WRITE'
```

put_last_list   Ai

Similar to the *put_last_structure* instruction but for lists. The following changes have been made to the *put_list* instruction:

```
4    R_Gpos          <-- my_gpos + 2
5    MODE            = 'WRITE'
6    R_RLGPOS        = 'YES'
```

5.3.3   Clause Head Instructions

get_value   An, Ai

This instruction represents a clause head argument that is a bound variable (i.e. the instruction is used when a variable occurs more than once as a formal clause argument). The instruction takes the value of argument register An and unifies it with the value of argument register Ai. This is one of the places where the complete unification routine is invoked.

```
1    UNIFY(An, Ai)
```

get_constant   C, Ai

This instruction represents a clause head argument that is a constant. The instruction unifies the value of register Ai against the constant 'C'. Variables with tag 'NEW_...' can be bound immediately. However, the binding of variables with tag '..._UNBOUND' has to be delayed until the processor has gained possession of the trail stack pointer. After having obtained the trail pointer the instruction is re-executed. (See the specification of the 'WAIT_UNTIL_SAFE' routine).

```
1    temp  <--  Ai
2    CASE  TAG.temp  OF
3       REF          : temp  <--  MEM(VALUE.temp)
4                      Goto 2
5       NEW_GLOBAL,
6       NEW_LOCAL  : MEM(VALUE.temp)  <--  <CONST|'C'>
7       GLOBAL_UNB : WAIT_UNTIL_SAFE(2,temp)
8                    TRAIL_GLOBAL(temp)
9                    MEM(VALUE.temp)  <--  <CONST|'C'>
10      LOCAL_UNB  : WAIT_UNTIL_SAFE(2,temp)
11                   TRAIL_LOCAL(temp)
12                   MEM(VALUE.temp)  <--  <CONST|'C'>
13      CONST      : IF  VALUE.temp <> 'C'  THEN  FAIL
14      OTHERWISE  : FAIL
15   ENDCASE
```

get_nil   Ai

This instruction represents a head argument that is the empty list. The instruction can be considered as a special case of the *get_constant* instruction; however, in this case the argument register Ai will be unified with a special constant, 'NIL', representing the empty list. If Ai cannot be unified with 'NIL', backtracking occurs.

```
1    temp  <--  Ai
2    CASE  TAG.temp  OF
3       REF          : temp  <--  MEM(VALUE.temp)
4                      Goto 2
5       NEW_GLOBAL,
6       NEW_LOCAL  : MEM(VALUE.temp)  <--  <NIL|_>
7       GLOBAL_UNB : WAIT_UNTIL_SAFE(2,temp)
8                    TRAIL_GLOBAL(temp)
```

```
9                       MEM(VALUE.temp)  <--  <NIL|_>
10    LOCAL_UNB  : WAIT_UNTIL_SAFE(2,temp)
11                      TRAIL_LOCAL(temp)
12                      MEM(VALUE.temp)  <--  <NIL|_>
13    NIL        : Continue
14    OTHERWISE  : FAIL
15    ENDCASE
```

get_void   Ai

This instruction represents a clause head void variable (i.e. a variable that does not occur anywhere else within the current clause).

```
1    CASE  TAG.Ai  OF
2       NEW_LOCAL : MEM( VALUE.Ai )  <--  <LOCAL_UNB|Ai>
3       NEW_GLOBAL: MEM( VALUE.Ai )  <--  <GLOBAL_UNB|Ai>
4       OTHERWISE : Continue
5    ENDCASE
```

get_structure   F, Ai

This instruction indicates the beginning of a structure (without embedded sub-structures) occurring as a clause head argument.

```
1    temp  <--  Ai
2    CASE  TAG.temp  OF
3       REF          :  temp  <--  MEM(VALUE.temp)
4                       Goto  2
5       NEW_GLOBAL,
6       NEW_LOCAL  : MODE  =  'WRITE_SAFE'
7                       Goto L1
8       LOCAL_UNB  : WAIT_UNTIL_SAFE(2,temp)
9                       TRAIL_LOCAL(temp)
10                      MODE  =  'WRITE'
11                      Goto L1
12      GLOBAL_UNB : WAIT_UNTIL_SAFE(2,temp)
13                      TRAIL_GLOBAL(temp)
14                      MODE  =  'WRITE'
15                      Goto L1
16      STRUCTURE  : IF  MEM(VALUE.temp) = F  THEN
17                          Nextarg  <--  VALUE.temp + 1
18                          MODE  =  'READ'
19                      ELSE  FAIL
```

```
20      OTHERWISE  : FAIL
21   ENDCASE

22   L1: GET_GPOS
23       MEM(VALUE.temp)    <--   <STRUCTURE|my_gpos>
24       MEM(my_gpos)  <--  F
25       Nextarg       <--   my_gpos + 1
26       my_gpos       <--   my_gpos + Arity(F)
```

get_last_structure   Ai,F

This instruction represents the beginning of the last structured object of a clause
head argument. The global stack pointer can therefore be relesed by this instruction. The following changes have been made to the *get_structure* instruction:

```
26   R_Gpos  <--  my_gpos + Arity(F)
27   R_RLGPOS   =   'YES'
```

get_list   Ai

This instruction is a special case of the *get_structure* instruction. The structure
in question is in this case a list.

```
1    temp  <--  Ai
2    CASE  TAG.temp  OF
3      REF         :  temp  <--  MEM(VALUE.temp)
4                     Goto  2
5      NEW_LOCAL  : MODE  =  'WRITE_SAFE'
6                     Goto L1
7      LOCAL_UNB  : WAIT_UNTIL_SAFE(2,temp)
8                     TRAIL_LOCAL(temp)
9                     MODE  =  'WRITE'
10                    Goto L1
11     GLOBAL_UNB : WAIT_UNTIL_SAFE(2,temp)
12                    TRAIL_GLOBAL(temp)
13                    MODE  =  'WRITE'
14                    Goto L1
15     LIST        : Nextarg  <--  VALUE.temp
16                    MODE  =  'READ'
17     OTHERWISE  : FAIL
18   ENDCASE

19   L1:  GET_GPOS
```

```
20    MEM(VALUE.temp)    <--  <LIST|my_gpos>
21    Nextarg            <--  my_gpos
22    my_gpos            <--  my_gpos + 2
```

get_last_list   Ai,F

This instruction represents the beginning of the last structured object of a clause head argument (in this case a list). The global stack pointer can therefore be relased by this instruction. The following changes have been made to the *get_list* instruction:

```
22   R_Gpos  <--  my_gpos + Arity(F)
23   R_RLGPOS   =  'YES'
```

5.3.4   Structure Instructions

unify_var   Vn

This instruction represents an unbound variable that occurs as an argument of a structure or list. When executed in 'WRITE_SAFE' mode variable Vn receives a "NEW_GLOBAL" tag and a pointer to the top of the global stack. If executed in 'WRITE' mode, a new variable is created on the global stack, and a reference to the new variable is stored in variable Vn. If the instruction is executed in 'READ' mode, the next argument of the structure being processed is obtained and stored in variable Vn.

```
1   CASE  MODE  OF
2      READ:  (Vn)       <--  MEM(Nextarg)
3             Nextarg <--  Nextarg+1
4      WRITE: MEM(Nextarg) <--  <GLOBAL_UNB|Nextarg>
5             (Vn)       <--  <REF|Nextarg>
6             Nextarg    <--  Nextarg+1
7      WRITE_SAFE:
8             (Vn)       <--  <NEW_GLOBAL|Nextarg>
9             Nextarg <--  Nextarg+1
10   ENDCASE
```

unify_xy_var   Ai,n

This instruction is an optimized version of the *unify_var* instruction. The new variable is simultaneously stored in the current environment (offset n) and in the argument register Ai. A clause head variable that is used by the first subgoal and latter goals is a frequent occurrence. Hence, the variable is loaded into an argument register but must also be stroed in the current environment.

```
1    CASE MODE OF
2       READ: MEM(my_env+n)  <--  MEM(Nextarg)
3             Ai             <--  MEM(Nextarg)
4             Nextarg        <--  Nextarg+1
5      WRITE: MEM(Nextarg)   <--  <GLOBAL_UNB|Nextarg>
6             Ai             <--  <REF|Nextarg>
7             MEM(my_env+n)  <--  <REF|Nextarg>
8             Nextarg        <--  Nextarg+1
9   WRITE_SAFE:
10            Ai             <--  <NEW_GLOBAL|Nextarg>
11            MEM(my_env+n)  <--  <NEW_GLOBAL|Nextarg>
12            Nextarg        <--  Nextarg+1
13   ENDCASE
```

unify_unsafe_value   Vn

This instruction represents a variable that is a structure or list argument but whose value might not necessarily exist yet on either the local or global stack. If the instruction is executed in 'READ' mode, the next argument of the structure currently being processed is read and unified with the variable Vn. If the instruction is executed in 'WRITE' or 'WRITE_SAFE' mode and variable Vn is a pointer with tag 'NEW_GLOBAL' a variable with tag 'GLOBAL_UNBOUND' is created at this address, and a reference with tag 'REF' to this location is pushed onto the stack. Remember, a pointer with tag 'NEW_...' points to an undefined location. When a reference to this location has to be created the referenced unbound variable must be brought into existence. If the value of variable Vn is a pointer with tag 'NEW_LOCAL' a new variable with tag 'GLOBAL_UNBOUND' is pushed onto the global stack and the location pointed to by Vn will be set to reference this newly created variable. If variable Vn dereferences to an unbound variable, the same action as above takes place (of course, the variable itself does not need to be brought into existence). Otherwise, the value of variable Vn is pushed onto the global stack.

```
0     GET_TPOS      /* Only necessary if Vn is an environment
                                    variable */
1     CASE  MODE  OF
2        READ:UNIFY( (Vn), MEM(Nextarg) )
3             Nextarg  <--  Nextarg+1
4        WRITE_SAFE,
5        WRITE:
6             temp  <--  (Vn)
7             CASE  TAG.temp  OF
8               REF:
9                   temp  <--  MEM(VALUE.temp)
10                  Goto 6
11              NEW_LOCAL:
12                  MEM(Nextarg)        <--  <GLOBAL_UNB|Nextarg>
13                  MEM(VALUE.temp) <--  <REF|Nextarg>
14                  Nextarg             <--  Nextarg+1
15              NEW_GLOBAL:
16                  MEM(VALUE.temp) <-- <GLOBAL_UNB|temp>
17                  MEM(Nextarg)        <--  <REF|temp>
18                  Nextarg             <--  Nextarg+1
19              LOCAL_UNB:
20                  WAIT_UNTIL_SAFE(6,temp)
21                  MEM(Nextarg)  <--  <GLOBAL_UNB|Nextarg>
22                  MEM(VALUE.temp)  <--  <REF|Nextarg>
23                  TRAIL_LOCAL(temp)
24                  Nextarg             <--  Nextarg+1
25              GLOBAL_UNB:
26                  WAIT_UNTIL_SAFE(6,temp)
27                  MEM(Nextarg)  <--  <REF|temp>
28                  Nextarg          <--  Nextarg+1
29              OTHERWISE:
30                  MEM(Nextarg)  <--  temp
31                  Nextarg          <--  Nextarg+1
32          ENDCASE
```

unify_value   Vn

This instruction represents a bound variable that occurs as an argument of a structure or list. In contrast to the *unify_unsafe_value* instruction, the value of variable Vn is guaranteed to exist; however, the value might be 'UNBOUND'. If executed in 'READ' mode the instruction gets the next argument of the structure currently being processed and unifies this argument with the value of variable Vn. If executed in 'WRITE' or 'WRITE_SAFE' mode the instruction pushes the value of variable Vn onto the global stack. However, if the value was of type 'NEW_LOCAL', 'NEW_GLOBAL', or 'REF' the variable must be dereferenced because in this case the variable refers indirectly to another variable whose value must be obtained. The only difference between the *unify_unsafe_value* and the *unify_value* instruction is in the treatment of the 'NEW_...' variables.

```
0    GET_TPOS      /* Only necessary if Vn is an environment
                                    variable */
1    CASE  MODE  OF
2      READ:UNIFY( (Vn), MEM(Nextarg) )
3            Nextarg  <--  Nextarg+1
4      WRITE_SAFE,
5      WRITE:
6            temp  <--  (Vn)
7            CASE  TAG.temp  OF
8              NEW_LOCAL,
9              NEW_GLOBAL,
10             REF:
11                temp  <--  MEM(VALUE.temp)
12                Goto 7
13             LOCAL_UNB:
14                WAIT_UNTIL_SAFE(7,temp)
15                MEM(Nextarg)  <--  <GLOBAL_UNB|Nextarg>
16                MEM(VALUE.temp)  <--  <REF|Nextarg>
17                TRAIL_LOCAL(temp)
18                Nextarg           <--  Nextarg+1
19             GLOBAL_UNB:
20                WAIT_UNTIL_SAFE(7,temp)
21                MEM(Nextarg)  <--  <REF|temp>
22                Nextarg       <--  Nextarg+1
23             OTHERWISE:
24                MEM(Nextarg)  <--  temp
25                Nextarg       <--  Nextarg+1
26             ENDCASE
```

unify_void

This instruction represents a structure argument that is a single occurrence variable. When executed in 'READ' mode, the current argument of the structure being read is skipped. If the instruction is executed in 'WRITE' or 'WRITE_SAFE' mode, it pushes a new unbound variable onto the global stack.

```
1   CASE MODE OF
2      READ:  Nextarg  <--  Nextarg + 1
3      WRITE_SAFE,
4      WRITE: MEM(Nextarg)  <--  <GLOBAL_UNB|Nextarg>
5             Nextarg  <--  Nextarg + 1
6   ENDCASE
```

unify_const   C

This instruction represents a constant that occurs as an argument of a structure or list. If executed in 'READ' mode, the next argument of the structure currently being processed is read and unified with the constant 'C'. Otherwise the constant 'C' is pushed onto the global stack to become part of the structure that is being created.

```
1   CASE  MODE  OF
2      READ:  temp  <--  MEM(Nextarg)
3             CASE  TAG.temp  OF
4                REF: temp  <--  MEM(VALUE.temp)
5                     Goto 3
6                NEW_LOCAL,
7                NEW_GLOBAL:
8                     MEM(VALUE.temp)  <--  <CONST|'C'>
9                     Nextarg  <--  Nextarg+1
10               LOCAL_UNB:
11                    WAIT_UNTIL_SAFE(3,temp)
12                    MEM(VALUE.temp)  <--  <CONST|'C'>
13                    TRAIL_LOCAL(temp)
14                    Nextarg  <--  Nextarg+1
15               GLOBAL_UNB:
16                    WAIT_UNTIL_SAFE(3,temp)
17                    MEM(VALUE.temp)  <--  <CONST|'C'>
18                    TRAIL_GLOBAL(temp)
19                    Nextarg  <--  Nextarg+1
20               CONST:
21                    IF  'C' <> VALUE.temp  THEN  FAIL
22                    ELSE  CONTINUE
```

```
23                          Nextarg  <--  Nextarg+1
24              OTHERWISE:  FAIL
25      WRITE_SAFE,
26      WRITE:  MEM(Nextarg)  <--  <CONST|'C'>
27              Nextarg       <--  Nextarg+1
28   ENDCASE
```

unify_nil

This instruction is a special case of the UNIFY_CONSTANT instruction described above. The constant in this case is the special constant 'NIL', representing the empty list.

5.3.5 Clause Control Instructions

try   n, Label

This instruction reserves space for a choice point on the local stack. It updates the choice point pointer to correspond to the new choice point, saves the program counter ,PC, and branches to the clause referenced by 'Label'.

```
1   Backtrack_Status         =    'SHALLOW'
2   R_Last_chpnt,my_chpnt   <--  LPOS
3   Buffer(SIZE)            <--  n
4   L_LPOS, R_LPOS         <--  LPOS + n
5   Nextclause             <--  pc
6   COPY_CHPNT              =    'YES'
7   pc                      <--  Label
```

retry   Label

This instruction represents a clause to be tried when previous clauses could not solve the current goal. However, if the current clause is also the last clause to consider, the *trust* instruction must be used.

```
1   Backtrack_Status =    'SHALLOW'
2   Nextclause       <--  pc
3   IF  COPY_CHPNT='NO'  THEN
4       MEM(my_chpnt.nextclause)  <--  Nextclause
5   R_Last_chpnt     <--  my_chpnt
6   pc               <--  Label
```

trust   **Label**

This instruction represents the last clause that might be applicable to solve the current goal. The choice point will be deallocated because there are no other choices for the current goal. The backtrack_status is set to deep, indicating that should the unification fail again, backtracking to some previous goal must take place.

```
1   Backtrack_Status        =   'DEEP'
2   COPY_CHPNT              =   'NO'
3   R_LPOS,L_LPOS          <--   my_chpnt
4   my_chpnt,R_Last_chpnt <--   Last_chpnt
5   pc                     <--   Label
```

switch_on_term   **LV, LC, LL, LS**

This instruction provides access to a group of clauses with a non- variable in the first head argument. It causes a dispatch on the type of the first argument of the call. The argument A1 is dereferenced and, depending on whether the result is a variable, constant, list, or structure, the program counter Pc is set to LV, LC, LL, or LS, respectively.

```
1   temp  <--    A1
2   CASE  TAG.temp  OF
3      REF       :  temp  <--  MEM(VALUE.temp)
4                   Goto 2
5      UNBOUND  :  pc <--  MEM(pc)
6      CONST,NIL:  pc <--  MEM(pc+1)
7      LIST     :  pc <--  MEM(pc+2)
8      STRUCTURE:  pc <--  MEM(pc+3)
9   ENDCASE
```

switch_on_constant   N, TABLE

This instruction provides hash table access to a group of clauses having constants in the first head argument position. Register A1 holds a constant whose value is hashed to compute an index in the range 0 to N-1 into the hash table. The hash table entry gives access to the clause or clauses whose keys hash to that index. The hash table is allocated in the code segment following the current instruction. Hence, the program counter pc points to the base of the hash table. The size of the hash table is N, which should be a power of 2. I assume that A1 does not hold the constant C itself, but rather a unique pointer to the value of the constant. Since all constants and ASCII strings have to be stored in a symbol table, the index of the constant in the symbol table can be used as the constant's hash value. Therefore the hash value of every ASCII string can be determined at compile time and does not have to be recomputed at run time.

```
1   temp  <--  A1 MOD N
2   IF  TAG.temp=REF  THEN
3       temp  <--  MEM(VALUE.temp)
4       Goto 2
5   pc    <--  MEM(pc + MEM(VALUE.temp))
```

switch_on_constant   N, TABLE

This instruction provides hash table access to a group of clauses having structures in the first head argument position. The effect is identical to that of SWITCH_ON_CONSTANT, except that the key used is the principal functor of the structure.

5.3.6   Fork/Join Instructions

fork   n, Label

This instruction examines a global semaphore to find out whether it is possible to execute the next two goals in AND-parallel fashion. If no resources are available, execution proceeds sequentially. Otherwise, execution delays until the left neighbor processor has terminated - this is necessary to prevent fails from the left neighbor from interfering with the fork operation. It is very difficult to reset two independent processes. In the current environment we enter a number to indicate how many processes have been spawned. Since *fork* is a binary operator, this number will always be two. Then the right neighbor is provided with a new set of stack pointers taken from a global stack pointer pool. Those stack pointers will constitute the environment in which the new process will execute. (Checking the 'stack_free' semaphore and setting it to 'NO' must be an indivisible operation).

```
1    IF   stack_free = YES   THEN
2         stack_free = NO
3         Wait until L_DONE = YES
4         MEM(my_env+n)  <--   2
5         R_Lpos  <--  new_local_stack_pointer
6         R_Gpos  <--  new_global_stack_pointer
7         R_Tpos  <--  new_trail_stack_pointer
8         PC      <--  Label
9    ENDIF
```

next_process

This instruction prepares the parallel execution of the next goal. It opens a new pipeline buffer block in the right pipeline buffer and provides a new environment in which the next process can be executed.

```
1    increment right buffer block
2    R_Lpos    <--  new_local_stack_pointer
3    R_Gpos    <--  new_global_stack_pointer
4    R_Tpos    <--  new_trail_stack_pointer
5    R_Currenv <--  my_env
```

end_fork

This instruction terminates the fork operation. It saves all the current stack pointers and continues identically to the *Stop* instruction.

join   n

This instruction implements the join operation. When a process returns to the join instruction, it is checked whether all parallel processes have terminated now. This fact is indicated by the fork count in the current environment (the number that was set by the *fork* instruction). If this count is zero, all parallel processes have terminated, the old stack system is restored, and execution proceeds with the next instruction following the join. Otherwise, the fork count is decremented and the stack pointers of the terminated process are returned to the global stack pointer pool. Then the processor resets itself and waits for the next goal to be processed. (Checking and decrementing the fork count must be an indivisible operation).

```
1    Wait until L_DONE = 'YES'
2    temp  <--  MEM(my_env+n)
3    temp  <--  temp - 1
4    IF  temp > 0  THEN
5       MEM(my_env+n)  <--  temp
6       return stack pointers to the global pool
7       stack_free  =  YES
8       reset_left_buffer
9       increment_left_block_count
        --------------------------
10      PC  <--  L_Entry
11      R_Currenv, my_env        <--  L_Currenv
12      R_Last_chpnt, my_chpnt  <--  L_Last_chpnt
13      R_Lpos                   <--  L_Lpos
14   ENDIF
15      restore old stack system
```

5.3.7 Miscellaneous Instructions and Micro-Operations

release_tpos

This instruction releases the trail stack pointer. However, if the processor is not in possession of the trail stack pointer it cannot be released but must first be obtained from the left neighbor. In order not to delay execution by waiting until the left neighbor has released the stack pointer - which might happen if we try to read the trail pointer and it is not there - a pipeline status flag, L_RLTPOS, is examined which indicates whether the trail pointer is available. If the trail pointer is available it is read and immediately relased, i.e. passed to the right neighbor. Otherwise, a processor status flag is set to indicate that the trail pointer is not needed by this processor. When the trail pointer becomes available later on, an interrupt will be issued to copy the trail pointer to the right neighbor. In other words, the processor status RELEASE_TPOS=YES together with the pipeline status L_RLTPOS=YES will cause an interrupt in the current processor to transfer the trail pointer from the left to the right pipeline buffer.

```
 1    IF  IN_POSESSION_OF_TPOS='YES'  THEN
 2        R_Tpos  <--  my_tpos
 3        R_RLTPOS  =  'YES'
 4    ELSE
 5        IF  L_RLTPOS='YES'  THEN
 6            R_Tpos  <--  L_Tpos
 7            R_RLTPOS  =  'YES'
 8            IN_POSESSION_OF_TPOS  =  'YES'
 9        ELSE
10            RELEASE_TPOS  =  'YES'
11        ENDIF
12    ENDIF
```

release_gpos

This instruction is identical to the above instruction but works on the global stack pointer.

trail_global(var)

This micro-routine checks whether a variable on the local stack needs to be trailed. Only those variables that lie before the last choice point need to be trailed. If the variable needs to be trailed it is pushed onto the trail stack.

```
1    IF   VALUE.var < my_chpnt   THEN
2         MEM(my_tpos)  <--   var
3         my_tpos          <--   my_tpos+1
4    ENDIF
```

trail_global(var)

This micro-routine checks whether a global variable needs to be trailed.

```
1    IF   VALUE.var < L_Gpos   THEN
2         MEM(my_tpos)  <--   var
3         my_tpos          <--   my_tpos+1
4    ENDIF
```

fail

This instruction resets all status flags to their default values and calls the appropriate fail routine.

```
1     RESET_RIGHT_NEIGHBOR
2     R_PROCEED    =   'YES'
3     R_RLTPOS     =   'NO'
4     R_RLGPOS     =   'NO'
5     L_RLTPOS     =   'YES'
6     L_RLGPOS     =   'YES'
7     RELEASE_TPOS  =   'NO'
8     RELEASE_GPOS  =   'NO'
9     CASE  BACKTRACK_STATUS  OF
10       SHALLOW:  SHALLOW_FAIL
11       DEEP   :  DEEP_FAIL
12    ENDCASE
```

shallow_fail

This instruction loads the PC with the address of the next clause to consider, untrails the variables and copies the environment pointer, the choice point pointer and the local stack pointer from the left to the right pipeline buffer. Note that if the processor does not possess the trail stack pointer it cannot have trailed any variables, hence it does not need to check whether it should untrail variables.

```
1    PC   <--   L_Nextclause
2    IF  IN_POSSESSION_OF_TPOS='YES'  THEN
```

```
3       temp  <--  R_Tpos
4       IF  temp <> my_tpos  THEN
5           my_tpos  <--  my_tpos-1
6           temp2    <--  MEM(my_tpos)
7           MEM(VALUE.temp2)  <--  temp2
8       ENDIF
9    ENDIF
10   R_Currenv     <--  L_Currenv
11   R_Lpos        <--  L_Lpos
12   R_Last_chpnt  <--  my_chpnt
```

deep_fail

When a 'deep fail' has occurred a choice point needs to be copied from the local stack into the left pipeline buffer to restore a previous machine state. After this has been done we proceed as in the 'shallow fail' case.

```
1    Wait until  L_DONE='YES'
2    copy choice point from local stack
3    into right pipeline buffer block
4    COPY_CHPNT = 'NO'
5    SHALLOW FAIL
```

reset

This instruction resets a processor to its initial state. It then tries to read another entry address to continue executing (Line 11). The processor will be idle until an entry address has been provided by the left neighbor.

```
1    RESET_RIGHT_NEIGHBOR
2    R_PROCEED                =  'YES'
3    R_RLTPOS                 =  'NO'
4    R_RLGPOS                 =  'NO'
5    RELEASE_TPOS             =  'NO'
6    RELEASE_GPOS             =  'NO'
7    IN_POSESSION_OF_TPOS     =  'NO'
8    IN_POSESSION_OF_GPOS     =  'NO'
9    COPY_CHPNT               =  'NO'
10   BACKTRACK_STATUS         =  'DEEP'
11   pc                       <--  L_Entry
12   my_env, R_Currenv        <--  L_Currenv
13   my_chpnt, R_Last_chpnt   <--  L_Last_chpnt
14   R_Lpos                   <--  L_Lpos
```

5.3.8 Built-in Predicates

Arithmetic built-in predicates are compiled in-line using standard arithmetic instructions. Meta calls such as assert, retract, clause, or name are not handled by the Prolog machine since those predicates cannot be expressed in Prolog and do not operate on Prolog structures. These predicates will cause a trap and the Prolog machine will hand them to the host computer to be processed. However, the cut operation will be supported through a special instruction and can be executed in-line.

first_cut

This instruction represents the 'cut' operator when the 'cut' occurs prior to any proper subgoal in the clause body. In this case only the last choice point pointer needs to be reset. However, the pointer to the choice point that was in effect when the current procedure was entered is still contained in the left pipeline buffer.

```
1   my_chpnt, R_Last_chpnt  <--  L_Last_chpnt
```

cut   n

This instruction represents a 'cut' operator that occurs after a proper subgoal within the clause body. The choice point that was in effect when the procedure was entered is restored and the top of the local stack is adjusted (i.e. all choice points and environments on top of the current environment are discarded and the stack space is released). The parameter 'n' is the size of the current environment

```
1   GET_TPOS
2   my_chpnt, R_Last_chpnt  <--  MEM(my_env+2)
3   R_Lpos          <--  MEM(my_env+n)
```

6 Simulation

6.1 Introduction

To evaluate the pipelined Prolog machine the execution of a set of benchmark programs (Appendix A) was simulated on a register transfer level. It is clear from the global system architecture (Figure 3-1) that the shared bus will eventually prove to be the bottleneck of the system. Various ways to configure the system were qualitatively investigated to find the optimal system configuration. The following configurations were considered (Figure 6-1a...6-1c):

1. A single shared memory which contains both the data and code space.

2. Separate data and code memories shared by all processors and accessed via independent busses.

3. Shared data memory and local instruction memories (i.e. every processor possesses a copy of the static part of the code).

Each of these configurations was analysed using the memory access time of the global memory module(s) as a simulation parameter.[21] It is obvious that a sequential Prolog machine would also benefit from having a separate data and instruction bus and/or faster memory access time to increase the memory bandwidth. A qualitative analysis of the various configurations must therefore also include a comparison of the pipeline machine with a sequential reference machine. This will allow us to measure how much of the gain in execution speed is due to the pipeline execution model and how much is due to the employment of faster memories and multiple busses. One could also refer to the faster memory (i.e. access time equal to the processor cycle time) as a cache. There exist very detailed studies of the cache behavior of compiled Prolog programs based on the Warren abstract machine [Ti85]. These studies include such parameters as cache organization, cache size, write back policy, cache block size, etc.; the results can be used to scale the results according to the cache organization employed. However, as memory chips get faster and cheaper a point will be reached where the cache can be replaced by a complete memory module. The simulation is detailed enough to take into account the bus conflicts on the data and instruction busses, and the complete fetch, decode, and execute cycle of each instruction simulated.

6.2 Simulated Hardware Structures

In order to perform a meaningful register transfer simulation the hardware structures to be simulated must be specified with an appropriate level of detail. The

---

[21]A memory access time equal to the processor cycle time and a memory access time twice the processor cycle time were considered.

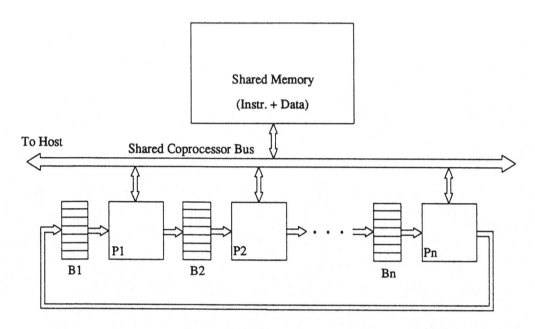

Figure 6-1a: Data and Instructions Shared in a Global Memory

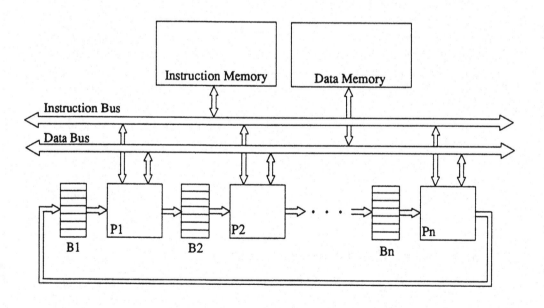

Figure 6-1b: Separate Data and Instruction Memories

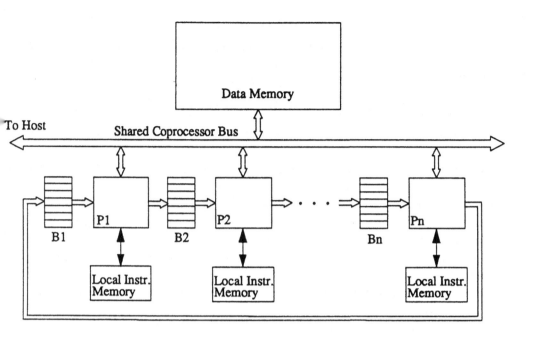

Figure 6-1c: Shared Data Memory and Local Instruction Memory

global system architecture and the configuration possiblities have been discussed in the previous chapter. We will now concentrate on the design of the individual processing elements of the pipeline.

Each pipeline stage consists of a pipeline buffer and a complete instruction set processor to execute the instruction set specified in Chapter 5. To obtain maximum performance the processor itself is internally pipelined, i.e. instructions are fetched, decoded, and executed in a pipeline fashion. To support this internal pipelining the processor consists of a logically independent instruction fetch/decode unit and an execution unit. The design of these units will now be discussed with the exception of the micro-instruction sequencer. Appropriate pipelined sequencers are commercially available.

The following sections describe the structure and the functionality of the main hardware modules of the parallel Prolog machine. The description is detailed enough to allow a realistic register transfer simulation of the parallel Prolog machine. However, the following sections do not claim to be a gate level specification for an actual hardware implementation. Rather, they provide the basis upon which a hardware design can be carried out. Undoubtedly the experienced hardware designer will be able to optimize the design without changing the functional requirements.

94

6.2.1 Pipeline Buffer

The logical structure of a pipline buffer is shown in Figure 6-2. It is always the left buffer which belongs to the processor. The pipeline buffer is organized as a dual port memory and consists logically of a fixed number of blocks with 32 entries per block. The left processor is called the producer and the right processor is the consumer due to the unidirectional data flow through the pipeline. When processes are executed in parallel it is possible that the producer passes information into a different block than the block from which the consumer currently reads. The blocks are addressed via a 3 bit counter. The blocks will always be worked on in a strict sequential order, i.e. after having worked on block i the block counter will be incremented to point to block i+1 modulo the number of blocks, i.e. having reached the end we will go back to the first block. One block contains all the information necessary to execute a Prolog goal. The entries within a block are accessed through a 5 bit offset register whose value is concatenated to the block address.[22] Access to the entries of a buffer block is restricted as follows: an entry can only be read after it has been written into. No further restrictions are required. Note that under this loose restriction it is possible to write several times into the same location without having read from this location. It is also possible to successfully read several times from the same location after it has once been written into. This considerably simplifies the implementation. When a particular block entry is written into, a semaphore flag will be set enabling reading from this location. This flag will stay set until the consumer processor is done with this block and proceeds to work on the next buffer block. At this time the semaphores for all the 32 block entries will be reset, disabling any read operation. It is assumed that this reset operation of all the flags can be accomplished within one machine cycle. Note that every buffer block has its own set of semaphores.

From Figure 6-2 we can also see how the processors are reset should a fail occur. When a processor executes a Prolog fail operation all its right hand neighbors must be reset (see Chapter 3.2.1). How is one to know when 'right' will become 'left' in a circular pipeline arrangement, i.e. how do I find the 'head' of the computation? The answer is simple: one only needs to compare the pipeline block addresses of the producer and consumer. If producer and consumer address both the same block then the consumer needs to be reset should the producer fail. Otherwise only the producer's current right buffer block will be reset, thereby effectively disabling the right processor to later become the consumer of the failing process. The status of each buffer block is described through four status bits (see Chapter 5.2).

---

[22]The decision to have 8 blocks with 32 entries each is arbitrary and was only motivated by technological reasons and cost. Of course, the offset register will be a regular 8 bit register but only the 5 least significant bits are used.

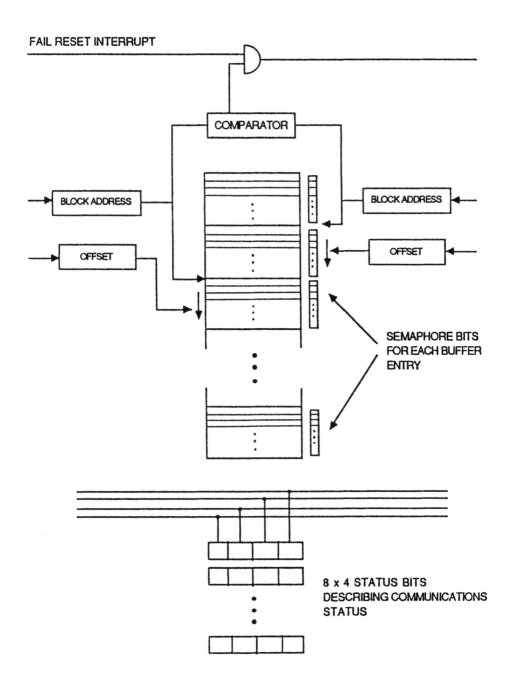

FAIL RESET INTERRUPT

COMPARATOR

BLOCK ADDRESS

BLOCK ADDRESS

OFFSET

OFFSET

SEMAPHORE BITS
FOR EACH BUFFER
ENTRY

8 x 4 STATUS BITS
DESCRIBING COMMUNICATIONS
STATUS

Figure 6-2: Structure of the Pipeline Buffer

6.2.2 Execution Unit

The structure of the processor execution unit including the pipeline buffer is shown in Figure 6-3. The primary design goal of the execution unit was simplicity, feasibility and maximum performance given these constraints. The execution unit basically consists only of a small (32x32) internal multi-port register file and a 32 bit ALU. The instruction unit, to be discussed in section 6.2.3, provides the instruction operands in two separate operand registers, op1 and op2. The whole performance of the system is derived from the judicious design of the data paths within the processor and of an efficient processing of data tags. The data paths shown in Figure 6-3 are highly optimized towards executing the instruction set specified in Chapter 5. External data can be read into the processor either from the pipeline buffer or from the shared data bus (via the memory data register, MDR). At either of those data paths a tag decoder PLA decodes the most significant 5 bits (the tag) of the 32 bit data word. The data tag, the op-code of the current instruction, and the processor status flags determine the micro-instruction to be executed next. Note that many instructions transfer data objects that are either not tagged, absolute addresses for example, or whose tags are not relevant for the current instruction. In those cases the decoding of the upper 5 bits is either supressed or ignored by the sequencer. Similarily, when data are to be written onto the shared bus or into the pieline buffer a tag generator generates the appropriate tag as required by the current instruction, i.e. the most significant 5 bits of the data word will be changed. If absolute values are written no tags are generated and the 32 bit data word is transferred unchanged.

To demonstrate the level of detail at which the simulation was conducted we shall now look at the actual simulation routine of the 'put_list' instruction specified in Chapter 5. The following routine is an actual listing taken from the simulator:

```
put_list(Ai)
 int Ai;

{INSTR = "put_list";

 {GET_GPOS;
  get_operand1(Ai);
  write_right_buffer( LIST(my_gpos),Ai);
  Nextarg = my_gos;
  GotoNext}

 {my_gpos = my_gpos+8;
  MODE  = Write;
  End_of_Instr}
}
```

At first the processor has to obtain the stack pointer to the global stack since it wants to create a list cell on the stack. If the processor is already in possession of

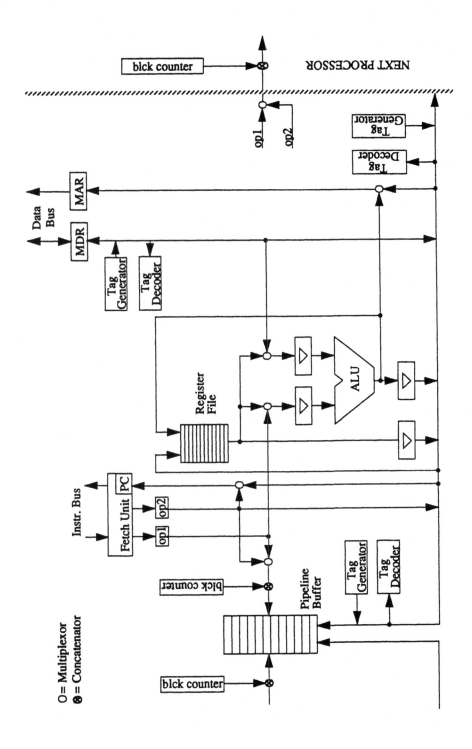

Figure 6-3: Structure of the Execution Unit

the stack pointer execution proceeds immediately. This is already determined at instruction decode time. The decoder uses the status flag "In_possession_of_gpos" to branch to the appropriate micro-instruction sequence. If the processor does not yet possess the global stack pointer, the micro-routine GET_GPOS tries to read the pointer from the left pipeline buffer. If the stack pointer is in the pipeline buffer this will require one machine cycle. Otherwise the processor will enter a wait state until the stack pointer is released by the right neighbor. Similarily the processor tries to obtain the operand of the instruction, which is the address of the argument register to receive the list pointer. If the operand has not been loaded into the op1 register by the instruction fetch unit, the execution unit enters a wait state. When the operand becomes available it will immediately be used to address the respective argument register of the right pipeline buffer block.[23] Simultaneously the value of the internal register my_gpos will be put on the data path to the right pipeline buffer and the tag generator will tag this data object as a list pointer (tag LIST). The value of my_gpos is also fed back into the multi-port register file to initialize the register Nextarg. This completes one cycle. At the next cycle register my_gpos is incremented by 2 and the processor mode is set to WRITE mode. This terminates the instruction. Therefore, if the processor is already in possesion of the global stack pointer and the instruction fetch unit has provided the instruction's operand, the instruction itself can execute in two machine cycles. This is only possible due to the special data paths and the use of many specialized status bits during the decoding of the instruction. For this reason it is not useful to employ commercial micro-processors (even micro-programmable processors). They lack the capability to handle the many status bits and most importantly they do not provide the highly optimized data paths. However, rather than using bit slice technology one should employ a commercial 32 bit ALU and 32 bit register files.

6.2.3 Instruction Fetch Unit

The instruction fetch unit is a logically independent unit. Its logical structure is shown in Figure 6-4. It consists of an instruction buffer two words deep, a set of multiplexors, an instruction decoder PLA, and two operand registers in which to align the instruction operands. The instruction fetch is complicated by the fact that the instructions are byte aligned. Only the destination addresses of jumps, branches, and calls must lie on word boundaries (i.e. every sequential code sequence must begin on a word boundary). When execution of a sequential code sequence begins, the instruction buffer is empty. As long as the instruction buffer is not full and instruction fetch is not disabled the fetch unit attempts to fill the buffer. As soon as the first buffer word has been filled the decode unit

---

[23]This is why there is a direct independent data path from the operand registers to the address registers of the pipeline buffer.

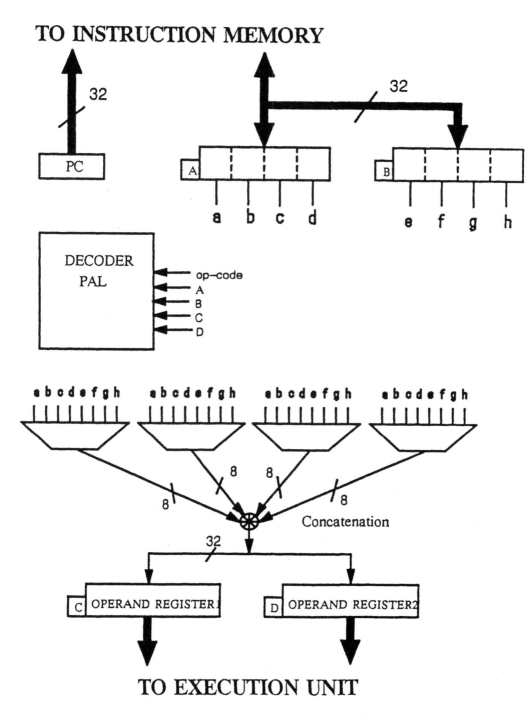

Figure 6-4: Structure of the Instruction Fetch/Decode Unit

extracts the first instruction op-code, which must lie on a word boundary. The op-code determines how many operands the instruction has and what their sizes are. The decode unit extracts the operands from the instruction buffer and loads the respective operand registers. This is done sequentially, i.e. for an instruction with two operands we will first extract one operand and then the other, even if both operands are available in the instruction buffer.[24] Then the decode unit will start all over again extracting the next op-code, which does not necessarily lie on a word boundary anymore. If an operand extends over a word boundary the decode unit will automatically delay extraction of the operand until the next instruction word has been loaded into the instruction buffer. Similarly, if an operand of a previous instruction still occupies a particular operand register, the new operand cannot be loaded into the respective operand register. This is implemented by providing each of the four registers (2 instruction buffer registers + 2 operand registers) with hardware flags indicating whether the respective registers are empty or full.

6.3 Simulation Results

The results of a comparative performance analysis between the parallel Prolog machine and a sequential reference architecture are shown in Figures 6-5a...6-5f). The parallel machine is represented by the dark shaded bars and the sequential machine by the lightly shaded bars. The sequential reference machine is based on the same instruction set, execution unit, and instruction fetch/decode unit as the parallel Prolog machine. However, all communication and synchronization overhead was stripped from the machine and the pipeline buffer has been replaced by a second internal register file to speed up the sequential machine. All possible compilation optimizations to speed up the execution of the sequential reference machine were utilized. Of course, most instructions of the parallel Prolog machine cannot be executed on a sequential machine. Those instructions were re-designed to work optimally on a sequential machine. Hence, in fact, two optimized instruction sets were designed - one for a parallel and one for a sequential machine. Both machines allow for different software and compiler optimizations but are based on comparable hardware structures. In particular the new treatment of unbound variables (Chapter 4) was also employed for the sequential instruction set. Actually this worked slightly against the parallel execution model. The variable classification scheme was originally developed to relax the synchronization requirements of the parallel Prolog machine. Only afterwards was it found that this method also considerably improves the execution time. Had the sequential machine been based on the old execution model the comparative performance of the parallel machine would have been much more impressive. Columns 1 through 6 of Figure 6-5 correspond to the various system configurations described earlier.

---

[24]Extracting an operand and loading it properly aligned into one of the operand registers is done through a set of multiplexors controlled by the decoder.

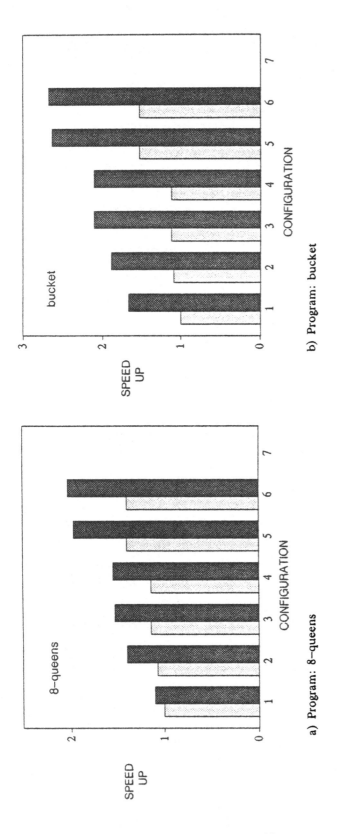

Figure 6-5: Pipeline Machine versus Sequential Machine

Column 1: Single Shared Memory (250 ns access time)
Column 2: Separate Instruction and Data Memories (250ns access time)
Column 3: Shared but Separate Instruction and Data Memories (125ns/250ns access time respectively)
Column 4: Local Instruction Memory and Shared Global Data Memory (125ns/250ns access time respectively)
Column 5: same as column 3 but with a faster data memory (125ns access time)
Column 6: same as column 4 but with a faster data memory (125ns access time)
Column 7: same as column 6 but utilizing mode declarations and AND-Parallelism where applicable

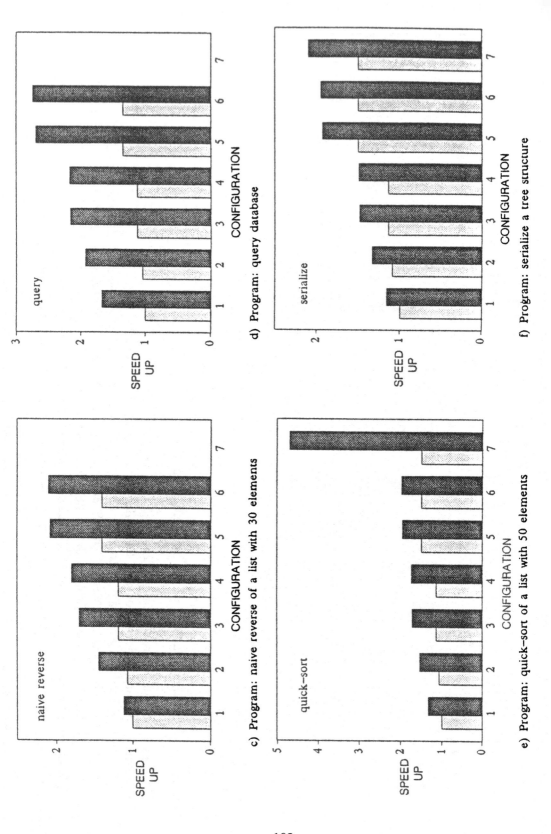

c) Program: naive reverse of a list with 30 elements

d) Program: query database

e) Program: quick-sort of a list with 50 elements

f) Program: serialize a tree structure

103

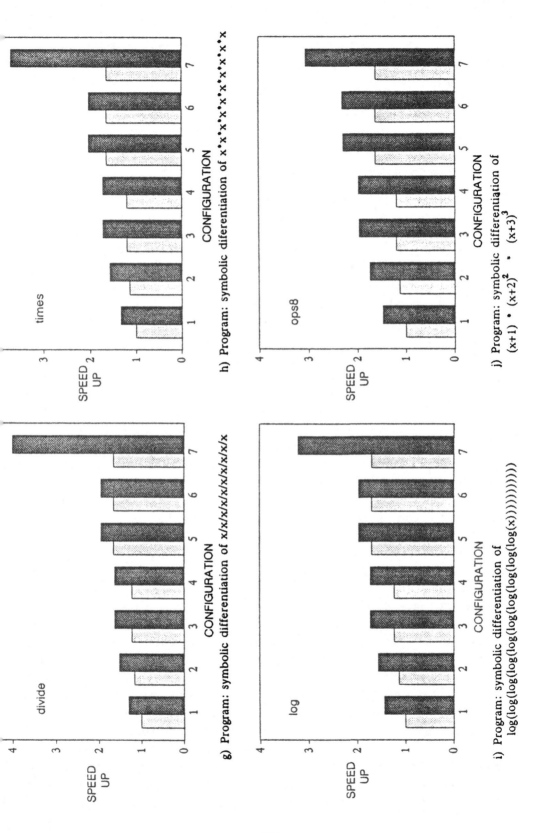

g) Program: symbolic differentiation of $x/x/x/x/x/x/x/x$

h) Program: symbolic diferentiation of $x*x*x*x*x*x*x*x$

i) Program: symbolic differentiation of
$\log(\log(\log(\log(\log(\log(\log(\log(x))))))))$

j) Program: symbolic differentiation of
$(x+1) * (x+2)^2 * (x+3)^3$

104

The extent to which a sequential machine benefits from the use of different configurations is also reflected in the results. The results are based on the following assumptions:

- processor cycle time 125ns

- shared memory access time 250/125ns

- local memory access time 125ns

As mentioned before, the fast memory can also be considered to be a cache. Hence, the results also indicate roughly how much can be gained by using a cache.

Column 7 shows how much additional performance can be obtained by utilizing mode declarations and exploiting restricted AND-parallelism; the system configuration is the same as in column 6. If no additional performance can be obtained the column has been left blank.

Except for column 7, all results are based on a parallel machine with a pipeline containing only 3 processors. In their standard execution mode the programs do not contain enough inherent parallelism to be able to keep more than three processors busy. For column 7 a five stage pipeline was employed. For all programs analysed the parallel machine is in all configurations superior to the sequential machine, even for programs that are highly deterministic and consist only of goals with very few arguments, e.g. naive reverse. The results also clearly show how important it is to provide mode declarations, either automatically derived or user provided, to further improve the performance (Figure 6-5e,g,h,i,j column 7). Interesting is the comparison between columns 3 and 4 (5 and 6). Column 3 (5) represents a configuration with a shared instruction memory whereas column 4 (6) represents a configuration where each processor has its own local instruction memory. Due to the conflicts on the instruction bus one would expect a performance increase if the instructions were to be moved into local instruction memories. However, as long as there are only three processors in the pipeline there is for most programs no measurable effect by doing so. The two-word instruction buffer, the compactness of the byte alligned code, and the average time it takes to execute an instruction guarantee that the instruction fetch unit has enough time to reload the instruction buffer without causing any wait states. We will now see how this is drastically changed as the number of processors in the system is increased. To keep the increasing number of processors busy, six parallel executing programs were injected into the pipeline. Of course, the performance of the system will strongly depend on the programs being executed. Rather than executing a mix of six different programs three simulation runs were executed. In the first run six naive reverse programs were executed in parallel, in the second and third run six quicksort and six 8-queens programs, respectively, were run in parallel (Figure 6-6a,b,c). The number of processors range from 1 - 8. The cycle time assumptions are the same as those made earlier. Figure 6-6 shows clearly that to reach maximum performance the processors must be provided with local

105

instruction memories. With only three processors in the system it does not matter much whether the code is fetched from a shared cache or from local memory (the same result obtained from Figure 6-5); however, with additional processors the instruction bus becomes quickly saturated and the performance curve becomes asymptotic. Figure 6-6 also shows that the system in maximal configuration (a shared data memory and local instruction memories with a 125ns access time) can support up to 8 processors accessing a shared data memory (cache) without too much performance deterioration due to data bus conflicts. For deterministic programs and with enough parallelism the system can easily provide a throughput in the 1 MegaLIPS range.

Given this maximal configuration I investigated the performance range of the system for different values of the system parameters. The results were compared with the benchmark performance of a micro- program implementation of the Warren instruction on a VAX 8600 and the PLM [Ge87]. The PLM is a sequential Prolog machine developed at the University of California/Berkeley [Do85]. The PLM executes with a cycle time of 100ns and the VAX 8600 has a cycle time of 80ns. Table 6-1 sumarizes the results. Table 6-1 also contains the benchmark performance of the Quintus Prolog compiler running on a SUN III Workstation with a MC68020 (20MHz) processor. For this comparison I did not use mode declarations or AND-parallelism to speed up execution. This would have been unfair, since the other system might have also benefitted from mode declarations. Entries for which no performance results could be obtained were left blank. The Japanese Personal Sequential Inference Machine (PSI) executes the deterministic append at 30 KLIPS; a complete benchmark performance list was not available [Yo83]. The new PSI II is reported to execute at a peak rate of 300 KLIPS (append) and an average performance of 100 KLIPS. The PSI II is also based on the Warren abstract instruction set. Generally it can be said that micro programmable machines like the VAX or the Symbolics LISP machines can execute compiled Prolog programs at a peak rate of roughly 100 KLIPS, whereas high performance sequential Prolog processors reach between 200-300 KLIPS.

One final question concerns the load distribution within the pipeline. Multiprocessor systems take great pains to guarantee uniform load balancing. It is obvious that directly recursive programs such as append, naive reverse, etc. will flow through the pipeline in a uniform manner. However, programs generally do not show such a uniform structure. Especially programs with many 'fails' cannot be expected to run smoothly through the pipeline because every 'deep' fail will completely flush the pipeline, which then has to be filled again. This will, of course, reduce the processor utilization. However, it will not cause the load distribution to become too unbalanced. This could only happen if the 'fail' were to repeatedly occur on the same processor. That is, if the program 'fails' exactly every nth unification, where n is the lenght of the pipeline. A very unlikely event for large programes. Table 6-2 shows the processor utilization on a 8 processor pipeline. The programs shown in Table 6-2 were selected because they exhibit

106

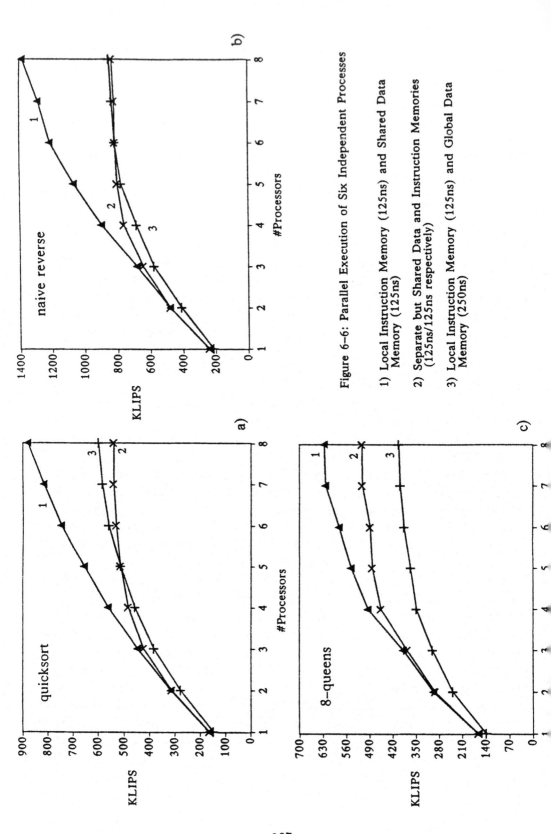

Figure 6-6: Parallel Execution of Six Independent Processes

1) Local Instruction Memory (125ns) and Shared Data Memory (125ns)

2) Separate but Shared Data and Instruction Memories (125ns/125ns respectively)

3) Local Instruction Memory (125ns) and Global Data Memory (250ns)

pipeline machine				VAX	PLM	SUN
machine cylce	60ns	60ns	100ns	100ns	80ns	100ns	50ns
data access	120ns	120ns	100ns	200ns	—	—	—
local memory	60ns	120ns	100ns	100ns	—	—	—
append	950	855	653	567	108	185	55
naive reverse	905	807	632	543	131	185	50
qsort	362	336	246	217	107	121	17
8-queens	488	455	380	293	94	75	21
serialize	275	264	217	165	79	95	16
query	249	236	190	150	101	123	8
times	271	251	190	162	51	54	12
divide	223	211	160	134	43	47	12
log	352	320	240	211	59	61	—
ops8	299	272	209	179	65	69	—
average	437	401	312	262	84	102	24

Table 6-1: Benchmark Performance in KLIPS

program	quicksort	8-queens	bucket
processor 1	19.9%	26.0%	18.9%
processor 2	20.5%	27.0%	18.1%
processor 3	19.2%	26.4%	22.1%
processor 4	19.2%	25.7%	19.5%
processor 5	19.6%	26.1%	21.3%
processor 6	18.3%	25.7%	17.3%
processor 7	17.7%	26.3%	18.5%
processor 8	19.1%	25.9%	21.0%

Table 6-2: Processor Utilization and Load Balancing

many 'fails' (shallow and deep). The purpose of Table 6-2 is not to show the overall processor utilization but rather the load balancing. For those particular programs the processor utilization cannot be very high because the programs 'fail' frequently and they do not exhibit enough parallelism to keep an eight processor pipeline busy. However, it can be seen that all processors are utilized at about the same level.

7 Conclusion

7.1 Contributions

The main contribution of this research was the development of a pipelined execution model for compiled sequential Prolog. This execution model allows for the parallel unification of several Prolog goals without violating the semantics of sequential Prolog. The execution model does not require any syntactic or semantic extensions of the language and fully supports sequential Prolog. The execution model was implemented in an abstract Prolog machine instruction set. The Prolog machine instructions are executed on a novel circular pipeline architecture of instruction set processors. Prolog specific synchronization requirements are kept to a minimum and are handled in a uniform way. The architecture has the advantage that a considerable part of the overhead of executing Prolog programs can be done in parallel with useful computation. In order to reduce the memory conflicts caused by the multi-processor pipeline, a Prolog variable classification scheme was developed, that, for all practical purposes, also solves the occur-check problem. The system is also capable of utilizing a restricted form of AND-parallelism. Another advantage of the architecture is the complete modularity. The system works with any number of processors in the pipeline (including just one). The performance of the system depends only on how much parallelism a particular Prolog program exhibits. However, even completely deterministic programs like 'append' or 'naive reverse' can be mapped onto the pipeline architecture and be executed faster than on an optimized sequential machine.

7.2 Future Work

Future work to be done includes, of course, the hardware realization of the parallel Prolog machine. It should also be investigated how to map parallel Prolog dialects like Concurrent Prolog, Parlog, and Guarded Horn Clauses onto the pipeline. This will probably involve designing a special instruction set to meet the requirements of those languages. Within the realm of sequential Prolog we will investigate to what extent we can relax the current restriction in the utilization of AND-parallelism.

A Benchmark Programs

This appendix lists all the benchmark programs that were used in this thesis. Except for programs 5) and 4) they are the benchmark programs proposed by D.H. Warren [Wa77/2]. They have been listed here for completeness sake:

1. Concatenation of two lists. The first list is a list with 30 elements to be concatenated with a list with one element.

   ```
   ?- append( List30, [1], R ).

   app([],X,X).
   app([H|T],X,[H|T2]) :- app(T,X,T2).
   ```

2. Naive reverse. A list with 30 elements is reversed.

   ```
   ?- nrev( List30, R ).

   nrev([],[]).
   nrev([H|T],X) :- nrev(T,Y), app(Y,[H],X).
   ```

3. Quicksort; a list with 50 elements is to be sorted. The list to be sorted is part of the benchmark program.

   ```
   List50 = [27,74,17,33,94,18,46,83,65, 2,
             32,53,28,85,99,47,28,82, 6,11,
             55,29,39,81,90,37,10, 0,66,51,
              7,21,85,27,31,63,75, 4,95,99,
             11,28,61,74,18,92,40,53,59, 8]

   ?- qsort( list50, R, [] ).

   qsort([],X,X).
   qsort([H|T],R,R0) :- split(T,H,Sm,Lrg),
                        qsort(Sm,R,[H|R1]),
                        qsort(Lrg,R1,R0).
   ```

```
split([],_,[],[]).
split([H|T],X,Sm,[H|Lrg]) :- X < H,!,split(T,X,Sm,Lrg).
split([H|T],X,[H|Sm],Lrg) :- split(T,X,Sm,Lrg).
```

4. The 8-queens problem (eight queens are to be placed on a chess board so
   that they don't attack each other.)

```
?-queens( [1,2,3,4,5,6,7,8], [], R).

queens( [], X, X ).
queens( List_to_select_from, Occupied_Positions, X ) :-
    select(List_to_select_from,Selected_Position,V),
    safe(Occupied_Positions,1,Selected_Position),
    queens(V,[Selected_Position|Occupied_Positions],X).

select( [X|Y], X, Y ).
select( [X|Y],Selected_Position,[X|V]) :-
    select(Y,Selected_Position,V).

safe( [], _, _ ).
safe( [U|T], N, Selected_Position ) :-
    nodiag( U, N, Selected_Position ),
    M is N + 1,
    safe( T, M, Selected_Position ).

nodiag( P, N, Selected_Position ) :-
    Occupied_down_diagonal is P + N,
    Selected_Position \= Occupied_down_diagonal,
    Occupied_up_diagonal is P - N,
    Selected_Position \= Occupied_up_diagonal.
```

5. This program solves a puzzle. There is a seven and a five liter bucket. By
   repeatedly filling, emptying, and pouring one bucket into the other, one is
   to reach a state where the seven liter bucket contains 4 liters and the other
   bucket is empty. Initially both buckets are empty. The program returns a
   list of cycle free state transitions from the start to the final state.

```
?- bucket( 4, 0, R ).

bucket(X,Y,Z) :- solve( s(0,0),s(X,Y),Z,[s(0,0),s(X,Y)] ).

solve( Start, End, [Start,End], States_visited ) :-
     reach(Start,End).
solve( Start, End, [Start|Tail], States_visited ) :-
     reach(Start,Next_state),
     not_element_of(Next_state,States_visited),
solve(Next_state,End,Tail,[Next_state|States_visited]).

element_of(X,[X|Y]).
element_of(X,[H|Y]) :- element_of(X,Y).

not_element_of(X,Y) :- element_of(X,Y),!,fail.
not_element_of(X,Y).

reach( s(X,Y), s(7,Y) ).
reach( s(X,Y), s(X,5) ).
reach( s(X,Y), s(0,Y) ).
reach( s(X,Y), s(X,0) ).
reach( s(X,Y), s(U,0) ) :- U is X+Y, U =< 7.
reach( s(X,Y), s(0,U) ) :- U is X+Y, U =< 5.
reach( s(X,Y), s(7,U) ) :- W is X+Y, W >= 7, U is W-7.
reach( s(X,Y), s(U,5) ) :- W is X+Y, W >= 5, U is W-5.
```

6. This program lexically orders the characters of an input list with the help
   of a binary tree. The return value is the lexical order sequence. The input
   list is part of the benchmark program.

```
?-serialize("ABLE WAS I ERE I SAW ELBA",X).

serialize(L,R) :-
    pairlists(L,R,A),
    arrange(A,T),
    numbered(T,1,N).

pairlists([X|L],[Y|R],[pair(X,Y)|A]) :- pairlists(L,R,A).
pairlists([],[],[]).
```

```
arrange([X|L],tree(T1,X,T2)) :-
    split(L,X,L1,L2),
    arrange(L1,T1),
    arrange(L2,T2).
arrange([],void).

split([X|L],X,L1,L2) :- !, split(L,X,L1,L2).
split([X|L],Y,[X|L1],L2) :- before(X,Y),!,
                                split(L,Y,L1,L2).
split([X|L],Y,L1,[X|L2]) :- before(Y,X), !,
                                split(L,Y,L1,L2).
split([],_,[],[]).

before(pair(X1,Y1),pair(X2,Y2)) :- X1 < X2.

numbered( tree(T1,pair(X,N1),T2),N0,N) :-
    numbered(T1,N0,N1),
    N2 is N1+1,
    numbered(T2,N2,N).

numbered(void,N,N).
```

7. This program symbolically differentiates simple algebraic expressions. The program is run with four different sets of input data. The input data are part of the benchmark program.

```
times10  = (((((((((x*x)*x)*x)*x)*x)*x)*x)*x)*x
divide10 = (((((((((x/x)/x)/x)/x)/x)/x)/x)/x)/x
log10    = lg(lg(lg(lg(lg(lg(lg(lg(lg(lg(x))))))))))
ops8     = (x+1) * (x**2 + 2) * (x**3 + 3)

d( U+V, X, DU+DV ) :- !, d( U, X, DU ), d( V, X, DV ).
d( U-V, X, DU-DV ) :- !, d( U, X, DU ), d( V, X, DV ).
d( U*V, X, DU*V+U*DV ) :- !, d( U, X, DU ), d( V, X, DV ).
d( U|V, X, (DU*V-U*DV)|V**2 ) :- !, d(U,X,DU), d(V,X,DV).
d(U**N,X,DU*N*U**N1 ) :- !,integer(N),N1 is N-1,d(U,X,DU).
d( -U, X, -DU ) :- !, d( U, X, DU ).
d( exp(U), X, exp(U)*DU ). :- !, d( U, X, DU ).
d( lg(U), X, DU|U ) :- !, d( U, X, DU ).
d( X, X, 1 ) :- !.
d( C, X, 0 ).
```

8. This program returns the solutions to a database query to find countries of similar population density.

```
?- query(X).

query([C1,D1,C2,D2]) :- density(C1,D1),
                        density(C2,D2),
                        D1 > D2,
                        20*D1 < 21*D2.

density(C,D) :- pop(C,P), area(C,A), D is (P*100)/A.
```

```
pop(china,      8250).        area(china,      3380).
pop(india,      5863).        area(india,      1139).
pop(ussr,       2521).        area(ussr,       8708).
pop(usa,        2119).        area(usa,        3609).
pop(indonesia,1276).          area(indonesia, 570).
pop(japan,      1097).        area(japan,      148).
pop(brazil,     1042).        area(brazil,     3288).
pop(bangladesh,750).          area(bangladesh, 55).
pop(pakistan,   682).         area(pakistan,   311).
pop(w_germany,  620).         area(w-germany,  96).
pop(nigeria,    613).         area(nigeria,    373).
pop(mexico,     581).         area(mexico,     764).
pop(uk,         559).         area(uk,         86).
pop(italy,      554).         area(italy,      116).
pop(france,     525).         area(france,     213).
pop(philippines,415).         area(philippines,90).
pop(thailand,   410).         area(thailand,   200).
pop(turkey,     383).         area(turkey,     296).
pop(egypt,      364).         area(egypt,      386).
pop(spain,      352).         area(spain,      190).
pop(poland,     337).         area(poland,     121).
pop(s-korea,    335).         area(s-korea,    37).
pop(iran,       320).         area(iran,       628).
pop(ethiopia,   272).         area(ethiopia,   350).
pop(argentina, 251).          area(argentina,1080).
```

B   Compilation Examples

This appendix provides three examples of compiled Prolog procedures using the parallel Prolog instruction set. The programs are the '8- queens' program, the 'quicksort' program, and one clause of the symbolic differentiation program. For all programs only the compilation of the top level procedure will be discussed. The quicksort program will serve as an example of how to use the 'fork/join' instructions to compile clause goals for AND-parallel execution.

In the following examples the left and right argument pipeline registers have been denoted L1..Ln and R1..Rn, respectively.

```
/*  queens( [], X, X ).
    queens( List_to_select_from, Occupied_Positions, X ) :-
         select(List_to_select_from,Selected_Position,V),
         safe(Occupied_Positions,1,Selected_Position),
         queens(V,[Selected_Position|Occupied_Positions],X). */
```

```
1    queens/3: switch_on_term(Lv,Lc,Ll,fail)

2    Lv:        try(11,Lc)
3               trust(Ll)

4    Lc:        proceed
5               release_gpos
6               get_nil(L1)
7               get_value(L3,L2)
8               release_tpos
9               complete_chpnt
10              stop


11   Ll:        allocate(6)
12              call(select/3,E1)
13              release_gpos
14              move(L1,R1)
15              put_var(2,R2)      * Selected_Position
16              put_var(3,R3)      * V
17              move(L2,4)         * Occupied_Positions
18              move(L3,5)         * X
19              release_tpos
20              stop
```

```
21   E1:        call(safe/3,E2)
22              release_gpos
23              move(4,R1)          * Occupied_Positions
24              put_const(R2,1)
25              put_value(2,R3)     * Selected_Position
26              release_tpos
27              stop

28   E2:        deallocate
29              execute(queens/3)
30              put_unsafe_value(3,R1)  * V
31              put_last_list(L7)
32              unify_value(2)          * Selected_Position
33              unify_value(4)          * Occupied_Position
34              move(L7,R2)
35              move(5,R3)              * X
36              release_tpos
37              stop
```

Line 1: Depending on the data type of the first argument of the current goal the 'switch' instruction will branch to label Lv (argument was of type variable), Lc (argument was of type constant or NIL), Ll (argument was of type list), or fail (the argument was a structure pointer). In this particular case allowing the first argument to be an unbound variable does not make any sense. However, the compiler does not know the semantics of the program and has to provide code for the worst case. Had the procedure been provided with a correct mode declaration the compiler would not have considered the case of an unbound variable as the first argument. Yet, given the type of the first formal argument of the involved clause heads the compiler can determine that an argument that is a structure pointer will invariably cause the procedure to fail.

Line 2: A choice point is created and space to accomodate the choice point is reserved on the local stack (11 words). Execution will branch to label Lc. Should the clause with label Lc not be able to solve the current goal, backtracking to the next clause takes place. The next clause is entered via a 'trust' instruction.

Line 3: The choice point created by the previous 'try' instruction is destroyed and execution branches to label Ll (i.e. the clause being entered by branching to label Ll is the last alternative to solve the current goal).

Line 4: Entry address of the first clause of procedure 'queens', i.e. queens([],X,X). Since the called clause is a unit clause we will immediately pass the return address to the right processor.

Line 5: The unit clause does not need the global stack pointer. Hence, the stack pointer of the global stack is released.

Line 6: Unify the empty list with the first argument of the caller.

Line 7: Unify the second and third argument of the calling goal.

Line 8: All possible bindings have been established by now. Hence, the local stack pointer can be released.

Line 9: The unit clause has been successfully processed. Copy the choice point contained in the left pipeline buffer into the local stack block reserved by the previous 'try' instruction. However, if the clause was entered directly without a previous 'try' instruction the 'complete_chpnt' instruction is interpreted as a NOOP instruction.

Line 10: Terminate the current code sequence. The current processor becomes idle.

Line 11: Entry address of the second clause of procedure 'queens'. An environment containing six words is allocated on the local stack.

Line 12: Call the first subgoal of the clause body. The return address is label E1.

Line 13: The clause head does not create anything on the global stack. Therefore the stack pointer can be released.

Line 14: The first argument of the first subgoal of the clause body is the same as the first argument of the clause head. Transfer this argument of the clause head to the right processor, where it will become the first argument of the next subgoal.

Line 15-16: Initialize the remaining argument registers of the first subgoal; in this case the arguments are unbound variables.

Line 17-20: Save the remaining clause head arguments in the current environment. Release the local stack pointer and terminate the current code sequence.

Line 21: Entry address of a new subgoal; call procedure 'safe/3' to solve the current goal. The return address is label E2.

Line 23: Restore an argument of the clause head. The clause head argument was saved in location 4 of the current environment and is now being loaded into the argument register R1 of the right neighbor.

Line 24: Load the constant '1' into the argument register R2.

Line 25: Load the value of a bound variable into register R3.

Line 28-29: Deallocate the current environment and call procedure 'queens/3' recursively to solve the last goal of the current clause body. Tail recursion optimization is applied in this case.

Line 30: Load the value of the variable 'V' from the current environment (which is the environment that was just discarded) into the argument register R1. Since, theoretically, the variable might still be unbound the variable needs to be relocated to the global stack. However, in this case the variable will always be bound to a nonvariable term. This value is copied into the argument register.

Line 31: Create a list cell on the global stack and store the new list pointer temporarily in register L7.

Line 32: The value of the head of the new list is the value of the variable 'Selected_Position'.

Line 33: The value of the tail of the new list is the value of the variable 'Occupied_Positions'.

Line 34: The list has been created. Now copy the list pointer into argument register R2, so that the next processor can work with the new list.

Line 35-37: Load the last argument into the appropriate argument register, release the stack pointer and terminate the current code sequence.

In the following example, quicksort, we will mainly discuss the compilation of clause body goals that can be executed in AND-parallel fashion. It is obvious that the two recursive calls of the program below are data independent and meet our critera for restricted AND- parallelism.

```
/*  qsort( [], X, X ).
    qsort( [H|T], R, R0 ) :-  split( T, H, Sm, Lrg ),
                              qsort( Sm, R, [H|R1] ),
                              qsort( Lrg, R1, R0 ).
*/
```

```
1  qsort/3:  switch_on_term( Lv, Lc, Ll, fail )

2  Lv:  try(11,Lc)        * create choice point and goto Lc
3       trust(L1)         * destroy choice point and goto Ll

4  Lc:  proceed           * beginning of clause qsort([],X,X)
5       release_gpos
6       get_nil(L1)
7       get_value(L3,L2)
8       release_tpos
9       stop              * end of clause qsort([],X,X)

10  Ll:  allocate(13)     * beginning of second clause
11       call(split/4,E1) * call first subgoal
12       get_last_list(L1)
13       release_tpos
14       unify_xy_var(R2,2)
15       unify_var(R1)
16       move(L2,3)       * save variable R
17       move(L3,4)       * save variable R0
18       put_var(5,R3)    * load new variable Sm into R3
19       put_var(6,R4)    * load new variable Lrg into R4
20       stop

21  E1:  fork(8,EP)

22       call(qsort/3,E2)
23       put_value(5,R1)  * load value of Sm into R1
24       move(3,R2)       * restore clause head argument R
25       put_last_list(L4) * create a list cell
26       unify_value(2)   * head of list is value of H
```

```
27          unify_var(7)          * tail of list is new variable R1
28          release_tpos
29          move(L4,R3)           * pass new list pointer to right
30          stop                  * neigbor and terminate

31   E2:    deallocate            * deallocate current environment
32          execute(qsort/3)      * tail recursive call to qsort
33          put_unsafe_value(6,R1)  * load value of Lrg into R1
34          release_gpos
35          put_value(7,R2)       * load value of R1 into R2
36          move(4,R3)            * restore head argument R0 in R3
37          release_tpos
38          stop

39   EP:    call(qsort/3,EP2)
40          put_value(5,R1)
41          move(3,R2)
42          put_list(L4)
43          unify_value(2)
44          unify_var(7)
45          move(L4,R3)

46          next_process

47          call(qsort/3,EP2)
48          put_unsafe_value(6,R1)
49          move(7,R2)
50          move(4,R3)
51          end_fork

52   EP2:   join(8)
53          deallocate
54          proceed
55          release_gpos
56          release_tpos
57          stop
```

Line 21: The fork instruction checks whether there are enough resources (i.e. whether there are free stack stystems) to spawn a new parallel process. If no new parallel process can be created, execution falls through the fork instruction and continues sequentially (lines 22 - 38). Note that no process will be queued.

However, if a new parallel process can be opened, the fork instruction branches to label EP.

Line 39: This is the beginning of the code for the parallel execution of the two recursive calls. All the code between line 39 and line 51 will be executed on the current processor. The first recursive goal and its arguments are passed to the right neighbor (line 39 to line 45). The return address of the goals to be executed in parallel is the address of the join instruction.

Line 46: The stack system is switched. Remember that the parallel processes have their own stack systems. Switching the stack system involves just re-assigning the stack pointers.

Line 47-51: The next goal and its arguments are passed to the right neigbor. The return address is again the join instruction. When the second goal has been dispatched the current processor becomes idle again.

Line 52-57: The join instruction waits until both parallel processes have terminated. The fork instruction has initialised a semaphore in the current environment. Every time a parallel process terminates and returns to the join operator the join instruction decrements the semaphore. When the semaphore becomes zero all parallel processes must have terminated, the current environment is discarded, and control returns to the parent clause. Note that by executing the recursive calls in parallel we had to give up tail recursion optimization. This is because control can not directly return from the bottom of the recursion to the parent clause but must go back to the respective join instruction.

In the following example a clause of the symbolic differentiation program has been compiled under the assumption that it is known that the first two arguments will always be used as instantiated input arguments and the third argument is an the output argument (mode declarations). In this case the structure (DU*V-U*DV)|V**2 will always have to be created. It is important to note that the structure components can in this case be created in an arbitray order as long as the final result conforms to the general 'layout' of Prolog structures (Figure B-1). The advantage of this optimization is that it is possible to establish the arguments for subsequent goals faster. The necessary clause control instructions for the complete differentiation program have been omitted.

```
/*  diff( U|V, X, (DU*V - U*DV)|V**2 ) :- !,diff( U, X, DU ),
                                           diff( V, X, DV).
*/
```

```
1          allocate(5)
2          get_structure(L1,|/2)
3          first_cut
4          call(diff/3,C1)
5          unify_var(R1)
6          unify_xy_var(L5,2)
7          move(L2,3)
8          move(L2,R2)
9          create_last_structure(L3,|/2,15)
10         c_var(8,R3)
11         c_var(4,4)
12         release_tpos
13         c_structure_pointer(14,12)
14         c_structure_pointer(13,3)
15         c_structure(12,-/2)
16         c_structure_pointer(11,9)
17         c_structure_pointer(10,6)
18         c_structure(9,*/2)
19         c_value(7,L5)
20         c_structure(6,*/2)
21         c_value(5,R1)
22         c_structure(3,**/2)
23         c_value(2,L5)
24         c_constant(1,2)
25         stop
```

```
26  C1:  deallocate
27       execute(diff/2)
28       move(2,R1)
29       release_gpos
30       release_tpos
31       move(3,R2)
32       move(4,R3)
33       stop
```

Line 2-4: The primary functor |/2 is matched against the first argument of the calling goal. If this match is successful the remaining unification must also succeed due to the invokation mode information. Hence the 'cut' operation can be performed immediately. (The 'cut' must always be delayed until a point is reached where no 'fail' in the current unification sequence can occur any longer). Since the 'cut' alters the Last_choice_point register of the right neighbor processor the call must occur after the 'cut'. This shows how important mode declarations are: to take full advantage of the architecture it is necessary to issue the call to the next goal as soon as possible. However, in clause bodies that start with a cut the first call has to be delayed until the 'cut' has been performed; hence, every attempt should be made to 'draw' the 'cut' into the clause head.

Line 9: The primary functor |/2 is pushed onto the global stack and enough space for the entire structure $(DU*V-U*DV)|V**2$ is reserved on the global stack, i.e. 15 words. The output variable contained in the argument register L3 is set to point to the new structure. Use of this instruction implies a priori knowledge that the structure will always have to be created. While the structure is created the components are accessed as a negative offset from the top-of-global-stack register. Structure components can now be created in an arbitrary order. NOTE: The lines 10 and 11 reflect why it is important to be able to create the structure components in an arbitrary order. The instructions in line 10 and 11 represent the variables DU and DV to be used as arguments in the following goals. It is important to have these arguments available as soon as possible. If the structure is built up in strict order the structure components DU and DV become available only much later.

Line 10: Load register R3 with a pointer to an unbound variable at location GPOS-8, as with a unify_var instruction in WRITE_SAFE mode the memory cell itself remains undefined.

Line 11: Load location 4 of the current environment with a pointer to an unbound variable at the location GPOS-4.

Line 13: Create a pointer (tagged 'STRUCTURE') to location GPOS-12 and store this pointer at location GPOS-14.

Line 15: Create the functor -/2 at location GPOS-12.

Line 19: Load the value of argument register L5 into location GPOS-7.

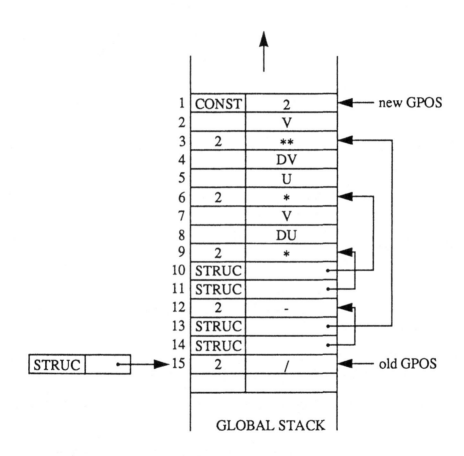

Figure B-1: Lay-out of the structure (DU*V-U*DV)/V**2

124

References

[AS87]   Ait-Kaci, H. and Smolka, G.: *Inheritance Hierachies, Semantics and Unification*, MCC Report, No. AI-057-87, Austin, Texas, 1987

[Br82]   Bruynooghe, M.: *The Memory Management of Prolog Implementations*, in Logic Programming, Clark and Tärnlund (eds.), Academic Press, 1982

[Ch85]   Chang, J.H.: *High Performance Execution of Prolog Programs Based on a Static Data Dependenciy Analysis*, Report No. UCB/CSD 86/263, University of California, Berkeley, October 1985

[Cl85]   Clocksin, W.F.: *Design and Simulation of a Sequential Prolog Machine*, New Generation Computing, Vol. 3, 1985, pp. 101-120

[CG86]   Clark, K., Gregory, S.: *PARLOG: Parallel Programming in Logic*, ACM Trans. on Programming Languages and Systems, Vol. 8, No. 1, 1986, pp. 1-49

[CK85]   Conery, J., Kibler, D.: *AND Parallelism and Nondeterminism in Logic Programs*, New Generation Computing, Vol. 3, 1985, pp. 43-70

[CL73]   Chang, C.L. and Lee, R.C.T.: *Symbolic Logic and Mechanical Theorem Proving*, Academic Press, 1973

[CM81]   Clocksin, W. and Mellish, C.: *Programming in Prolog*, Springer-Verlag, 1981

[Co73]   Colmerauer, A. et al.: *Un Systeme de Communication Homme-Machine en Francais*, Groupe de Recherche en Intelligence Artificielle, Université d'Aix Marseille, 1973

[Co82]   Colmerauer, A.: *Prolog and Infinite Trees* in Logic Programming, Clark and Tärnlund (eds.), Academic Press, 1982

[CT82]   Clark, K. and Tärnlund S.A. (eds.): *Logic Programming*, Academic Press, 1982

[Do85]   Dobry, T.P., et al.: *Performance Studies of a Prolog Machine Architecture*, Proceedings of the 12th Int. Symp. on Computer Architecture

[Ga85]   Gabriel, J., et al.: *Tutorial on the Warren Abstract Machine for Computational Logic*, Internal Report, Mathematics and Computer Science Division, Argonne National Laboratory, Illinois, 1985

[Ge87]   Gee, J., et al.: *Advantages of Implementing Prolog by Microprogramming a Host General Purpose Computer*, Proceedings of the 4th International Conference on Logic Programming, Melbourne, 1987

[GB77]   Giloi, W.K. and Berg, H.K.: *Introducing the Concept of Data Structure Architecture*, Proc. Int. Conf. on Parallel Processing, 1977, pp. 44-51

[Gr87]   Gregory, S.: *Parallel Logic Programming in Parlog*, Addison-Wesley, 1987

[It85]   Ito, N., et al.: *Data-flow Based Execution Mechanism of Parallel and Concurrent Prolog*, New Generation Computing, 3, 1985, pp. 15-41

[He30]   Herbrand, J.: *Researches in the Theory of Demonstration*, in *From Frege to Godel: A Source Book in Mathematical Logic, 1879-1931*, J. van Heijenoort (Ed.), Harvard University Press, 1967, pp. 525-581

[Ka86]   Kaneda, Y., et al.: *Sequential Prolog Machine PEK*, New Generation Computing, 4, 1986, pp. 51-66

[Kn86]   Knodler, B., Rosenstiel, W.: *A Prolog Processor for Warren's Abstract Instruction Set*, Microprocessing and Microprogramming 18, pp. 71-80, 1986

[Ko74]   Kowalski, R.: *Predicate Logic as a Programming Language*, Proceedings IFIP 74, North-Holland, 1974, pp. 569-574

[Ko83]   Kowalski, R.: *Logic for Problem Solving*, North-Holland, 1983

[Ku86]   Kursawe, P.: *How to Invent a Prolog Machine*, Proccedings of the Third International Conference on Logic Programming, Springer-Verlag, 1986

[Ll84]   Lloyd, J.W.: *Foundation of Logic Programming*, Springer-Verlag, 1984

[Me85]   Mellish, C.S.: *Some Global Optimizations for a Prolog Compiler*, Journal of Logic Programming, Vol. 1, 1985, pp. 43-66

[MM82]   Martelli, A. and Montanari, U.: *An Efficient Unification Algorithm*, ACM Transactions on Programming Languages and Systems, Vol. 4, No. 2, pp. 258-282, April 1982

[Mo82]   Mota-Oka, T. (Ed.): *Fifth Generation Computer Systems*, Proc. of the Int. Conf. on Fifth Generation Computer Systems, JIPDEC, North-Holland, 1982

[Na86]   Naish, L.: *Negation and Control in Prolog*, Lecture Notes in Computer Science, No. 238, Springer-Verlag, 1986

126

[N85]   Nolke, U.: *Prolog-Statistik*, Internal Report, Nixdorf Computer AG, June 1985

[On85]   Onai, R., et al.: *Architecture of a Reduction-Based Parallel Inference Machine: PIM-R*, New Generation Computing, 3, 1985, pp. 197-228

[On86]   Onai, R., et al.: *Analysis of Sequential Prolog Programs*, Journal of Logic Programming, Vol. 2, 1986, pp. 119-141

[PW78]   Paterson, M.S. and Wegman, M.N.: *Linear Unification*, Journal of Computer and System Sciences, 16, pp. 158-167, 1978

[Pl84]   Plaisted, D.A.: *The Occur-Check Problem in Prolog*, Int. Symp. on Logic Programming, Atlantic City, 1984, pp. 272-280

[Ro65]   Robinson, J.A.: *A Machine Oriented Logic based on the Resolution Principle*, Journal of the ACM, Vol. 12, No. 1, January 1965, pp. 23-41

[Sm86/1]   Smolka, G.: *Typed Equational Logic as a Programming Language*, SEKI-Report, Universität Kaiserslautern, 1986

[Sm86/2]   Smolka, G.: *Order-Sorted Horn Logic, Semantics and Deduction*, SEKI-Report, Universität Kaiserslautern, 1986

[Sh83]   Shapiro, E.Y.: *A Subset of Concurrent Prolog and its Interpreter*, Technical Report TR-003, ICOT, Tokyo, 1983

[Sh86/1]   Shapiro, E.Y.: *Systems Programming in Concurrent Prolog*, in *Logic Programming and its Applications*, D.H.D. Warren and M. van Caneghem (eds.), Ablex, 1986

[Sh86/2]   Shapiro, E.Y.: *Concurrent Prolog: A Progress Report*, in Fundamentals of Artificial Intelligence, W. Bibel and J.Jorrand (eds.), Lecture Notes in Computer Science, Vol. 232, Springer-Verlag, 1986, pp. 277-313

[Sh86/3]   Shapiro, E.Y.: *The Art of Prolog Programming*, MIT Press, 1986

[Sy85]   Syre, J. and Wetsphal, H.: *A Review of Parallel Models for Logic Programming Languages*, Technical Report CA-07, European Computer Research Center, Munich, Germany, 1985

[Ta86]   Tanaka, H.: *A Parallel Inference Machine*, Computer, Vol. 19, No. 5, May 1986

[Ti85]   Tick, E.: *Prolog Memory Reference Behavior*, Technical Report No. 85-281, Computer Systems Laboratory, Stanford University, September 1985

[TW83]   Tick, E. and Warren, D.H.D.: *Towards a Pipelined Prolog Processor*, Proc. of the Int. Symp. on Logic Programming, 1984, pp. 29-40

[Wa77/1] Warren, D.H.D.: *Implementing Prolog: Compiling Predicate Logic Programs*, Vol. 1, DAI Research Report No. 39, University of Edinburgh, May 1977

[Wa77/2] Warren, D.H.D.: *Implementing Prolog: Compiling Predicate Logic Programs*, Vol. 2, DAI Research Report No. 40, University of Edinburgh, May 1977

[Wa79]   Warren, D.H.D.: *Prolog on the DEC-System-10*, DAI Research Paper No. 127, University of Edinburgh, 1979

[Wa80]   Warren, D.H.D.: *An Improved Implementation Which Optimises Tail Recursion*, Proceedings of the Logic Programming Workshop, Debrecen, Hungary, July 1980

[Wa83]   Warren, D.H.D.: *An Abstract Prolog Instruction Set*, SRI Technical Report No. 309, Stanford Research Institute, October 1983

[Wi84]   Wise, M.J., Powers, D.M.W.: *Indexing Prolog Clauses via Superimposed Code Words and Field Encoded Words*, Symposium of Logic Programming, 1984, pp. 203-210

[Ue85]   Ueda, K.: *Guarded Horn Clauses*, ICOT Technical Report TR-103, Tokyo, 1985

[Ya86]   Yang, R.: *A Parallel Logic Programming Language and its Implementation*, Ph.D. Dissertation, Keio University, Japan, 1986

[Yo83]   Yokota, M., et al.: *The Design and Implementation of a Personal Sequential Inference Machine: PSI*, New Generation Computing, Vol. 1, 1983, pp. 125-144